Transforming Christian Theology

Advance praise for *Transforming Christian Theology*

"Philip Clayton is one of the world's leading philosophical theologians. In this new book, he calls for a transformation of theology—for a theology that transforms by radically engaging the concrete and practical concerns of both church and society. Pointing to significant movements within the Christian church, as well as shifts in late modern culture, Clayton clearly shows that the time is right for challenging old divisions such as 'evangelical' and 'liberal.' A welcome call for and contribution to transforming theology!"

F. LeRon Shults
Professor of Theology and Philosophy
University of Agder, Kristiansand, Norway
Author of *Reforming the Doctrine of God*

"In the confusion of how to live one's faith in these changing times, Dr. Clayton calls all of us, and especially young people, not to 'give up on church.' Thankfully, he goes on to tell us why and how, with a challenge to become active theologians, to write our own credos and debate them vigorously. That is the challenge he has taken up in this valuable book."

Bishop Mary Ann Swenson
The Los Angeles Area
The United Methodist Church

Transforming Christian Theology

For Church and Society

Philip Clayton

In collaboration with
Tripp Fuller

Fortress Press
Minneapolis

TRANSFORMING CHRISTIAN THEOLOGY
For Church and Society

Cover image: M.C. Escher's "Metamorphosis II (part of)" © 2009 The M.C. Escher Company-
Holland. All rights reserved. www.mcescher.com
Cover design: Paul Boehnke
Interior design: PerfecType, Nashville, Tenn.

Library of Congress Cataloging-in-Publication Data
Clayton, Philip, 1956-
  Transforming Christian theology : for church and society / Philip Clayton in collabora-
tion with Tripp Fuller.
     p. cm.
  Includes bibliographical references (p.   ).
  ISBN 978-0-8006-9699-3 (alk. paper)
  1. Theology, Doctrinal—United States. 2. Church and the world. 3. Church. I. Fuller,
Tripp. II. Title.
  BT30.U6C53 2010
  261'.10973—dc22
                                    2009035382

14 13 12 11 10   2 3 4 5 6 7 8 9 10

Contents

Part Three: Theologies That Can Transform Society

Part Four: Conversations Worth Having

Foreword

When I was a pastor—and had a pastor's expense account—I subscribed to the flagship magazine of liberal Protestantism and the flagship magazine of conservative Protestantism. I just wanted to keep up-to-date with both sides.

Each of these magazines has an editorial in each issue, in which the magazine weighs in on the issues of the day. After subscribing for a while, I started to play a game with myself. I'd read the headline and first couple sentences of the editorial, then guess as to the magazine's concluding position on the issue.

And you know what? I was right every time. I batted 1.000. No matter the issue, be it abortion rights, politics, immigration, cloning, health care, what have you, I could predict with perfect accuracy the position of the Christians on the left and the Christians on the right.

Of course, this was not due to my prophetic abilities. No, it is instead a testament to how predictable and, dare I say, stale American Protestantism has become. We know what the left will say, and we know what the right will say. So, what more is there to say?

A lot, it turns out. For just when the pundits are proclaiming the death of progressive Christianity, along comes Philip Clayton.

Philip's is an intellect par excellence, and he's got all of the letters after his name that gain him serious street cred in the liberal academy. Yet he cannot deny that his soul has been sprinkled with the spice of passionate evangelicalism. What this makes him is unpredictable (thanks be to God!).

In the following pages, you will find some items with which you wholeheartedly agree and others that will discomfit you. That's because you can't quite pin Philip down. He's a theologian, a scientist, and, I daresay, an evangelist. His gospel? Why, Jesus Christ, of course.

A thinking, feeling, studied understanding of Jesus Christ emerges from Philip's studies and his conversions (yes, there have been more than one). If that attracts you, then read on. If it discombobulates you, even more reason to read this book.

Ultimately, what Philip points out herein is what drew many of the leaders of the emerging church movement out of evangelicalism a decade ago: A desire for a robust, nuanced theology. One that can handle paradox. One that can be in sophisticated conversation with the best philosophers and scientists of our day. Indeed, that's what has drawn many emerging leaders to the progressive side of Christianity.

But what Philip and his intrepid Sancho Panza, Tripp Fuller, have found is that mainline Christianity has abdicated the one thing it has going for it: *theology*. So they're calling us all back to the one thing that can give rise to progressive Christianity's resurrection: theology, debate, Christology, doctrine. If there is to be a salvation of mainline Christianity, it will be theology. Indeed, it will be populist theology. I'm going to repeat that: *The salvation of progressive Christianity will be populist theology.*

I've spent time with some of the most renowned liberal Christian theologians of our day. Many fit the stereotype of "academic liberal" all too well. They are enamored of their own projects in Queer Theory, socialist economic models, and interfaith dialogue (not that there's anything wrong with that!). And they are, for the most part, completely uninterested in promulgating their ideas over the high walls of the academy (gasp!) by posting something on Facebook.

But some are like Philip and Tripp: They are passionate about bringing to light the story of Christianity that we, as progressive theologians, believe. It's a good version of Christianity. Some of us think it's the best version of Christianity. And we should stop hiding it under a bushel.

May this book be a first salvo in that effort.

Tony Jones is theologian-in-residence,
Solomon's Porch, Minneapolis, Minnesota
http://tonyj.net

Preface

Christian language is alive and well in the churches—and sometimes outside them as well. But deep reflection about this language is in trouble. These pages offer a radical call to pastors and laypeople to *transform* theology as we know it today. They're also a call to each reader to explore and voice his or her own Christian beliefs in such a way that they can have a *transforming* impact on both church and society.

What you are holding in your hand is not a book; it's the tip of an iceberg. Transforming Theology is a network of networks, a nationwide movement of people who are working to transform and renew the Christian church in and for the twenty-first century. Two Transforming Theology conferences are already scheduled for 2010, and we expect more to follow. The wealth of research, data, and proposals that inspired this call to action can be found at www.transformingtheology.org. Dozens of videoclips, YouTube posts, podcasts, short reflections, and more await you there. More are being added every day. We encourage you not only to watch and listen, to browse and download, but also to post your own reactions, links, and resources. Become part of the movement!

What you're about to read is not just meant for solo study. It's meant to spawn group discussions in your congregation, small group, cohort, or ministry group. To this end, Tripp Fuller has composed a series of integrated questions for "Conversations Worth Having" in part 4. We strongly urge you to sit down with friends and have these conversations. If you pastor a church or run a Christian organization, we hope you'll get your entire group involved in wrestling with this book and the urgent questions it raises. Then let us know as the new insights and programs begin to emerge.

Many around us are proclaiming that the church is dead and that core Christian beliefs are irrelevant in the contemporary world. We believe they are mistaken. But Jesus' message *will* be consigned to the dustbins of history unless we, together, begin to show why and how it remains relevant to our day. Just using Christian language and citing Scripture passages is not enough. Will you join us in transforming Christian theology, so that the power of the Christian message can again speak transformatively in the church and in the world?

The work of many brilliant theologians and committed church leaders stands behind these pages. Among many others, we thank: the Ford Foundation and Sheila Daveney, for their generous grant to support "rekindling theological imagination"; Marjorie Suchocki, my colleague and co-leader of the grant; the thirty theologians and the thirty denominational leaders who attended the two Claremont consultations in 2009 and whose wisdom gave rise to this book; the 140 bloggers (and growing) of the Transforming Theology blogging network; authors and practitioners in "emerging" churches, who get the challenges; Kate Clayton and the many other pastors whose innovative "best practices" are my inspiration; my collaborator, Tripp Fuller, who has dramatically increased the impact of the Transforming Theology movement; the band of young scholars and visionaries with whom I've been working at Claremont—Jeanyne Slettom, Andrea Stephenson, Deena Lin, Ashley Riordan, Eric Hall, Jeremy Fackenthal, and Benjamin Chicka; Jheri Cravens, who (once again) typed the manuscript; Michael West and his grand staff at Fortress Press, especially Susan Johnson, who saved me from a multitude of (editorial) sins; Judy and my children, who paid a price; and finally, to the One whom we seek to follow faithfully, without whose grace and self-emptying all of this would be nothing more than a noisy gong or a clanging cymbal.

Introduction:
Getting Clear on What You (Really) Believe

When I pick up a book, I wonder about the author: Who is she? What's her background? More importantly, I want to know: Why did he write this book? What does he have to tell me? What can I learn from him? Life is short, so I want to know these things up front. Presumably you do as well.

I'm writing this book because it seems that many Christians no longer know how to talk about their faith—at least not in an open, attractive, reflective, humble, inquiring, and truth-seeking way. It's not just that we don't know how to "witness"; we don't even know what we *ourselves* believe. I'm writing this book because I think that this is a very, very serious problem that needs to be addressed—now.

Maybe an anecdote will help you see what I mean. My last book, *Adventures in the Spirit: God, World, Divine Action* (Fortress Press, 2008), was published nine months ago, but I have yet to read any academic reviews of this work. That's because the world of academia grinds along slowly; it takes months for theologians to weigh in on new books and for major journals to start publishing reviews. But Pastor Bob Cornwall in Michigan is already blogging his way through my book. His thoughts, and my reactions, are being read by people across the country. In the new "space" of the Internet, people get to watch a theologian struggle over the criticisms of a parish pastor—in real time. When they have something to add, they click on "comment," and their thoughts instantly appear on the blog site next to mine. Author and readers are wrestling together, side by side, with the deep questions of our faith.

In a posting late last night, an auto mechanic in Idaho helped me learn something new about a school of thought called "process theology." I suddenly realized that we're not just talking about process theology; this *is* theology in process! What we're doing is being the church; we're thinking out loud together about the core issues of our faith. The questions are owned not by professional theologians but by everyday Christians. For example, Pastor Bob continues to push me, week after week, with an exhortation no one ever gave me during years of doctoral studies in theology: "But will it preach?"

The Internet and other new technologies have democratized theology in a way that no one could have imagined just a generation ago. Here's the byproduct: rather than lowering the standards for solid theology, these folks are raising the bar! It is a whole lot more difficult for us professionals to do theology in this new public arena than it once was to write theology books for the scholars who used to formulate the objections that we thought we had to answer. This book argues that there are urgent Christian reasons to give theology back to the churches and to ordinary people—even if the word *theology* has to be radically transformed in the process.

Professional theologians are not trained to pay a lot of attention to what ordinary Christians think. We dialogue mostly with other theologians and academics (sort of like God listening only to the angels). Traditionally, theology has been modeled on a Greek and medieval understanding of God. At its most extreme, this leads to the belief that God could not interact with the world without compromising God's omnipotence. Not all theologians accept this heritage, of course. Process theologians, for example, understand God as being universally responsive. God is "the Supremely Related One," according to Marjorie Suchocki.[1] God receives the responses of absolutely every created individual at every moment and then responds back to each individual in the very next moment with a divine "lure," calling him or her, in turn, to a God-like response. I believe it was this understanding of God—as One who listens to all and responds with infinite love to all—that was in play last night in the dialogue between a theologian, a Michigan pastor, and an auto mechanic from Idaho. Is this an improvement? You bet it is.

> *Doing theology is just thinking about your faith.*

You can already tell that this is meant to be a radically democratic book. We need to stop delegating theology to specialists and return it to the people who need it, the people whose right (and responsibility) it is to "just do it." *Doing theology is just thinking about your faith.* Theology therefore belongs to everyone who is drawn to Je__ wants to figure out what it means to be identified with him in this _erly complex, twenty-first-century world. (It's also harder than the old _theology—you could just memorize that kind, but you have to think _hen you do this kind.)

Actually, taking this step is more _ democratic move; it's a revolutionary move. Who knows what ordinar_stians might do if given permission to think deeply about what their f_mplies for themselves, for their local churches, and for all the other rol_t they play in society? I suspect that if we take an end run around acad_ theology and redefine theology to mean what ordinary believers think a_lk about, some powerful things will happen. I *am* certain, however, th_we don't, academic theology by itself won't be enough to carry the futu_ the church. And the thought of a church without individuals who as dis_s of Jesus think deeply about the burning issues of our day—about glob_arming and racism and science and religiously motivated warfare—is a_htening thought indeed.

Academic theology——the theology _t's done in seminaries and divinity schools and academic journals—isn't g_g to help us rethink what "church" means in this radically new world. I_act, most academic theologi_ans are hardly addressing the topic. How do_know? I know because until recently I was one of them. I specialized in _e most abstract kinds of theol_ gy one can do: theist metaphysics, philoso_ical theology, and the theology——science dialogue. It was only recently, as th_divorce between Church and A____cademy appears almost to be finalized, tha_finally saw the foolishness of _____y ways.

A Prophetic Challenge to Academic Theology

My Damascus Road experience was initiated by two great church ___thinkers: Brian McLaren and John Cobb. Two of Brian's books in particular, ____A Generous Orthodoxy (Zondervan, 2004) and Everything Must Change (Thomas Nelson, 2007), shook me to the core. In numerous publications ____and talks (many available as free downloads on iTunes), Brian has been calli_____g theologians and church leaders to recognize that this is a major time of ____transition and to take steps to lead the church through it. He argues—rightly—that this unique time places a special obligation on theologians to be "pa_____ssionately devoted to truth." [2]

I think Brian is exactly on track. Professional theologians, incl_____luding me, have needed to hear this call for a long, long while, and it's time_____e for us to take it fully to heart. Yet many of main hesitant to do so. Why? In part it's because theologians are trained classical languages and time-worn academic debates. Asking us to writing short, accessible blogs and to post videos on YouTube feels sking us to step out of the boat and walk on water. It is frightening erritory for professional theologians trained to write careful academic. Unfortunately, the complexity of our language (of which I was once oud!) means that we have enormous difficulty in communicating clearh and for the church.

In the end, it was the visiona ker John Cobb who played the decisive role in my conversion away purely academic theology. John calls the church to renewal and transfion in an amazing book that should be required reading for all theol tudents (as it is now for mine) and church people alike: *Reclaiming Church: Where the Mainline Church Went Wrong and What to Do a It.* In it, John argues that the chief obstacle to renewal and transformn in churches today is "the inability of the church to think theologically."[3] words are nothing short of prophetic: "There is . . . a lack of a shared sen of the primary importance of that to which the church witnesses. As long this sense is lacking, the church cannot convincingly call for primary col tment or loyalty. It must inevitably settle for third, four rth, fifth, or sixth ce in the priority system of most of its members" (8).

There are man causes for this mala, but John contends that the main problem is *the prof ssionalization of the*ogy: "The problem lies in the gap now existing betwe n theology and churn life, a gap that did not exist to any comparable ext nt a century ago" (23 The result is tragic: "Lay people and pastors do not inderstand themselves s responsible to think as Christians" (23). The prim ary responsibility for Christian thought now belongs to professors who teac in seminaries and divinity schools. For some centuries this worked, becaus theologians like me wrote books that helped clarify the mission of the ch urch, books that guided thinking Christians and church leaders, books that p rovided material for pastors as they prepared sermons and sought to bring t e word of God to life anew for their congregations. But over the last fifty year s or so things began to change. Theology evolved into another academic disc cipline, pursued according to academic standards and aimed at a largely aca demic audience. The upshot was predictable. According to John Cobb, "The ere is a tendency for seminary professors of theology to take less responsibility y for the ongoing development of theology. It suffices to be a good student and critic of theology, who can pass on to one's students a critical understanding of what theologians have said" (27).

Here's the problem: academic theologians, like me, are responsible for preparing candidates for ordination and for giving them the tools they need to pastor for the rest of their lives. If what we teach them is irrelevant to ministry in the real world, what will they do upon leaving seminary? As Cobb notes, they will "[fall] back on the popular notions they brought with them to seminary, only now knowing that these could not be taken seriously as 'theology'" (26). Ill-prepared to make connections between academic theology and faith in daily life, clergypersons often resort to offering combinations of native biblical understanding, pop psychology, and readings of "the signs of the times." In short, not only have seminaries not prepared future ministers well, but we also have unintentionally taken away from them the right to call whatever they *do* come up with "theology." We have not only failed to teach them to speak; we have cut out their tongues as well! The results can only be disastrous for the church as a whole: "Unless the Christian faith can provide the basis for assimilating the truth of the new challenges of the 20th century into a whole that is communicable to many, and unless Christians can point convincingly to what this new vision requires, oldline Protestantism will relapse more and more into lukewarmness—and death" (12f).

Toward the Rebirth of Theology

John Cobb's words have convicted me as strongly as anything in my life as a Christian. Reviewing what I was teaching to first-year seminary students, I realized I was still unconsciously teaching to standards internalized during my doctoral work. I was subjecting these future ministers to complex distinctions drawn from the history of theology or contemporary philosophy, but I was not showing them how these distinctions are relevant to today's world— if they even are! Most theologians leave ministry questions to instructors in the "arts of ministry"—preaching, pastoral counseling, worship, church administration, and the like. But that's just wrong. It's *my* responsibility as a theologian to help draw connections to the life of the church, and this responsibility cannot be shunted off on others.

For me, personally, the first step to "transforming Christian theology" was to change the way I teach. I now require my ministry students to develop a personal Credo—a statement of what they really believe—in response to the core questions of the Christian faith: Who is God? Who is Jesus? What is salvation? What is church? These detailed documents reflect their call to ministry, their understanding of the Scriptures, and the context in which they anticipate they will be ministering. I still introduce students to a variety of approaches to theology, of course, but now the goal is to help them glean insights from others about how to better articulate *their own* responses to the core questions of faith. Jesus asked of his disciples, "But who do you say that I am?" (Mt. 16:15). No one who has a call to Christian ministry gets to walk away from class without answering that question.

The second step in my transformation is to walk the talk, which means that I must also change how *I* communicate my reflections on Christian belief and identity. I can no longer publish theology books that are written primarily for specialists. From now on I must write for a broader audience, one that includes ordinary people who are eager to speak clearly and passionately of their faith—*and* those who are struggling to find out exactly what in the Christian story they really do care passionately about. In this regard, my last book represents the end of one era for me, and this book heralds the beginning of the next.[4] Perhaps this will irritate academic theologians and there may be backlash. But, as I've argued, the urgency of the situation calls for some pretty radical responses. We can't afford "business as usual" any longer.

The third and final step in my process of repentance is to become active in bringing about a sea change among academic theologians. With a grant from the Ford Foundation to "rekindle theological imagination," Marjorie Suchocki and I assembled a group of thirty leading theologians to talk about the problems and to look for ways professional theologians might do our work better so that it will have transformative influence on church and society. Two months later we invited thirty denominational leaders and leaders from the National Council of Churches to do the same. This book is an attempt to share with you the first results of what we are learning. We want to break the monopoly academic theologians have had on theology and to return serious Christian reflection to all who are drawn to walk the Way of Jesus. To change things, we have to understand why so many people have lost the ability to give powerful, vibrant accounts of what it means to be "Christian" in today's world and what it is they actually believe.

Many people are doing great stuff in congregations and in social ministries, and we should celebrate their work. But our *accounts* of what we're doing, and why we do it, often wouldn't earn a "pass" from my junior high Sunday school teacher. (Okay, she was pretty tough.) Christian action is alive and well in mainline churches, but Christian self-descriptions are in crisis. We have trouble talking about what is *uniquely Christian* about our lifestyles and ministries, and our inability is crippling those ministries. Laryngitis has attacked our vocal cords. This book is a call to give the church back its tongue, to help everyday Christians find their voices again.

Imagine what will happen when pew-sitting Christians and those who have gradually drifted away from the institutional church—together with pastors, denominational leaders, and directors of social justice ministries—begin to share their personal faith stories and talk openly and passionately about their faith journeys. Imagine a church where every member is thinking deeply about the core Christian questions in light of our contemporary world. Imagine congregations where everyone can address the hot-button issues of our day out of the deepest resources of the Christian tradition—perhaps haltingly, perhaps with some radically new types of answers, but still with humility and deep reflection. That's the goal of the Transforming Theology movement, of which this book is one expression.

Perhaps you're worried that if Christians start to talk about what they really believe, they'll begin splintering the church, and all hell will break loose (figuratively speaking). So I'm going to work equally hard in the coming pages to describe a *way* for folks to talk systematically about what they believe—that is, to begin doing theology—that is not dogmatic, divisive, or relativistic. I'll list the reasons why I think our culture is now undergoing a major paradigm shift that is opening up new ways of believing and talking. And I'll say why I think this is really good news for individual disciples, for the church, and for new modes of transformative Christian activism in society and in the world at large.

You may not associate doing theology with being revolutionary now, but by the time you've finished this book, I hope you will have changed your mind.

Part One

Theology for an Age of Transition

1. Things Have Changed,
or "Toto, We're Not in Kansas Any More"

O ver the last years all of us have watched the geography of the American church undergo a radical transformation. It's almost as if there has been a major earthquake—or, more accurately, a series of major earthquakes—realigning the entire landscape in which we live. It reminds me of pictures of the San Andreas Fault in California. On the west side of the fault line you can see an outcropping of rocks coming down the hill. On the east side of the line you see the rock ridge continuing on its way back up the other hill. The trouble is, the ridge on the east side is about a hundred yards further south from the one on the west—the entire land mass has rearranged itself. That's what many of us see as we look around American society today.

 Religion in America Fifty Years Ago

I wasn't an adult in the 1950s, so I can't speak from experience about the church in the post-war, Eisenhower era. But I can point you to a fantastic description of American religious life in the 1950s in the classic study by Will Herberg, *Protestant, Catholic, Jew*. In the vast majority of the communities that Herberg studied, people's Christian or Jewish identity was one of the very top items on their identity checklist. It stood up there with their patriotic identity as Americans (in fact, as in our day, the two were frequently confused with each other!). Especially if you lived in a smaller town, you would very likely have attended the same church that your parents had attended. Probably you would have been baptized and married in the same church, and you expected your funeral service to take place there in due course.

Not only that, but you would have shared most of your fundamental values in common with the others in your congregation. Since the vast majority of Americans were either Protestant, Roman Catholic, or Jewish there was a remarkable degree of consensus, and thus a relatively small range of choice. Your church or synagogue taught and reinforced your core values about faith, sex, family, politics—you name it. It was also the center of your social world. Two or three times a week Christians came to church to be together with other church people. Church social events stood at the center of your social life, and your life partner (for that's what marriages were expected to produce in those days) was very likely drawn from your broader church community.

Thus Herberg could write in 1955 that, "Almost everybody in the United States today locates himself in one of the three great religious communities. Asked to identify themselves in terms of religious 'preferences,' 95 per cent of the American people, according to a recent public opinion survey, declared themselves to be either Protestants, Catholics, or Jews."[1] It was not a great decade for free thinkers:

> Through the nineteenth century and well into the twentieth America knew the militant secularists, the atheist or "free-thinker," as a familiar figure in cultural life, along with the considerably larger numbers of agnostics who would have nothing to do with churches and refused to identify themselves religiously. These still exist, of course, but their ranks are dwindling and they are becoming more and more inconspicuous, taking the American people as a whole. The "village atheist" is a vanishing figure; Clarence Darrow and Bran the Iconoclast, who once commanded large and excited audiences, have left no successors. Indeed, their kind of anti-religion is virtually meaningless to most Americans today, who simply cannot understand how one can be "against religion" and for whom some sort of religious identification is more or less a matter of course.[2]

Herberg's data showed that church membership was growing twice as fast as the American population was. It was the Golden Age for the American church. But it was not to last long.

The '60s and '70s

We know the 1960s as a time of radical change, when huge transformations in beliefs and values began to take place. What is interesting about the early 1960s, however, is that, although values did begin to change, Christian and

Jewish communities continued to provide the primary point of orientation for most people. It was a time of revolutionary (and often confusing) transition within American culture, and yet for a long time people continued their high levels of involvement in churches and synagogues. It was well into the 1970s, or even later, before the cultural changes produced gaps between the people and their congregations, so that they gradually began identifying less with their traditional religious communities.

By the late 1960s and early 1970s, however—the period when I came of age religiously—there was a wide, almost disorienting range of religious options. My own story was perhaps not untypical for the time: I could continue to attend the mainline Presbyterian church that had been my church home since elementary school. I could attend an evangelical Bible study group associated with one of the evangelical churches in my area. I could attend a charismatic prayer meeting once a week, affiliated with a Pentecostal church. I could actually start attending the Assemblies of God church. Or I could make a community of "Jesus People" my Christian home, becoming a part of what would later be called the non-denominational or independent church movement. (In fact, over time I tried *all* these options—as many others were also doing.)

Having all these options to decide from was way more confusing than if I had been living in Ames, Iowa, or Bakersfield, California, in the 1950s! Still, note one feature of this choice: *all of these options were options in organized religion.* The option, "spiritual but not religious," was just beginning to appear on the map of American religious choice, but it involved at that time only a small percentage of the American public. In the early 1970s most of our real religious options were still "institutional" options.

 ## American Religion in the Early Twenty-First Century

Now fast forward to today. Surveys funded by the Pew Charitable Trust indicate an ever-increasing number of Americans are stepping outside of institutional religion altogether. You are probably already familiar with the steady decrease in membership in mainline churches. But did you know that, according to a recent U.S. Religious Landscape Survey, "the United States is on the verge of becoming a minority Protestant country"? According to the Pew Forum on Religion and Public Life, only 51 percent of Americans still report that they are members of Protestant denominations.[3] Evangelical

Protestant churches, together with historically black Protestant churches, make up 33.2 percent of the overall adult population, whereas mainline Protestant churches now represent only 18.1 percent of that population (5). Moreover, the "graying" of the mainline continues; roughly half the members of mainline churches are age fifty and older (9).

The 2008 Pew report also points out a new pattern: "the proportion of the population that is Protestant has declined markedly in recent decades while the proportion of the population *that is not affiliated with any particular religion* has increased significantly" (18, emphasis added). Throughout the period of the '70s and '80s, a constant 60 to 65 percent of respondents identified themselves as Protestant. The early '90s began a period of steady decline. By 2006 both the Pew survey and the General Social Surveys (GSS) found Protestant affiliation down to roughly 50 percent. Most of the overall decline is due to the rapid membership drop in the mainline churches. The Pew report notes, "What scholars who have analyzed the GSS data have found is that the proportion of the population identifying with the large mainline Protestant denominations has declined significantly in recent decades, while the proportion of Protestants identifying with the large evangelical denominations has increased" (18).

But the evangelical churches haven't been shielded from losses either. The publishing arm of the Southern Baptist Convention, LifeWay Christian Resources, reported recently that in 2007 "the number of people baptized in Southern Baptist churches fell for the third straight year," reaching "the denomination's lowest level since 1987," and "total membership dropped by nearly 40,000." In 2007 alone baptisms dropped nearly 5.5 percent.[4] Similar losses in other evangelical denominations are viewed with serious concern among leaders.

The grounds for these declines will occupy us throughout the coming pages. One obvious reason is that the range of religious options and identities has exploded for Americans today. Most of us know friends, colleagues, or acquaintances who are Christian, Jewish, Muslim; Buddhist, Hindu, Taoist; atheist, agnostic, "doubting believers"; pantheist, panentheist, neo-pagan; Mormon, Jehovah's Witness, Church of God; Bahá'í, Zoroastrian, perennialist—the list goes on and on. Faced with such a confusing array of options, more and more Americans are choosing not to choose. They develop "serial religious personalities," progressing gradually (or not so gradually) through a huge range of religious options, influenced by age, friends, geographic location, newspapers, or the most recent books they find in the Metaphysics section of their local bookstore. I think a lot of Americans feel like the six-year-old who finally convinces her parents to take her to Baskin-Robbins: it's so overwhelming to encounter that huge range of flavors that you just can't decide which one to try. Some try them all; others stop coming.

This bewildering multiplicity of religious (and non-religious) options is only the start for Christianity's new context. What it means to be church today, and what it will mean over the coming two to three decades, is affected just as strongly by the explosion of new technologies and the radically new forms of social networking that they create. Who could have imagined just ten years ago that millions of people would find their primary social home on a website? That we would spend more time on Facebook than on the phone? That millions of us would find our life partners through eHarmony.com? That the future of Iran would be significantly influenced by Twitter.com? That a president would be elected in no small part because of personal appeals posted on YouTube? First emailing, then texting, now tweeting and other new options are fundamentally transforming our social world. Religious identities by 2020—just a few short years away—will be determined by technologies that we can't even begin to imagine today.

Consider the role of Beliefnet.com. This amazing website and social networking center is now the go-to place for millions of Americans when they want to learn about religion, post personal thoughts and responses, or find religious community. Pastors and religious authorities no longer interpret the religious options for most Americans today, whether or not they still attend a church or synagogue; websites do. We can learn anything—and proclaim anything—directly on the Internet. If you are unsure about your religious identity, for example, just try the "Belief-O-Matic" function at Beliefnet.com. As the opening blurb proclaims:

> Even if YOU don't know what faith you are, Belief-O-Matic™ knows. Answer 20 questions about your concept of God, the afterlife, human nature, and more, and Belief-O-Matic™ will tell you what religion (if any) you practice . . . or ought to consider practicing. . . . (Warning: Belief-O-Matic™ assumes no legal liability for the ultimate fate of your soul.)[5]

No wonder people feel a little strange participating in a social arrangement called the "local congregation," a structure designed for the world of the eighteenth century, before there were cars or even light bulbs!

2. Do Christians Have to Hate Change?

As hard as it can be to cope with it, *change is good!* The stereotype says that until you're thirty you make change, and from thirty on you fight it. It's certainly true that older people tend to be in charge of organizations, and organizations are often the major blocks to change. But the stereotypes don't quite fit. There are people in their twenties who are trying to keep everything the same, and people over sixty who are in the forefront of change. (If you're not sure about this, go listen to John Cobb or Phyllis Tickle on YouTube sometime.) The question is: Should Christians view change as a bad thing?

I find nothing in the bewildering array of new choices and the ever-accelerating transformation of humanity and the planet that convinces me Jesus' message is no longer relevant or that attempting to follow Jesus' Way is antiquated and irrelevant. Quite the opposite: I suggest that the loss of traditional certainties is opening up access for more and more people to Jesus' words about the in-breaking kingdom of heaven and a "new wine" that simply can't be contained in old wineskins (Matt. 9:17). Karl Barth, the most famous Protestant theologian of the early twentieth century, famously described Christians as living *zwischen den Zeiten*—"between the times." We are a people on the way, a vagabond people, a people that are "in but not of" the world. Because our identity is not shaped *by* the world, we can live *for* it.[1] Our calling is to be a people who, in cooperation with God's Spirit, seek to bring about an order of love and justice that is clearly not the world we see around us.

Given this calling to join in God's reconciling mission, Jesus-followers are—to put it paradoxically—those who feel most at home when they are not at home. They are those who follow one who said, "Foxes have holes, and birds of the air have nests; but the Son of Man has nowhere to lay his head" (Matt. 8:20). We face the risk of complacency when those around us start telling us that the current world order is safe and secure and we should make ourselves at home in it. By contrast, when change is all around and the future feels unpredictable, the disciples of the Itinerate One should know that they are in their element.

Some decades ago—long enough that I won't get anyone in trouble for telling the story now—some students at a major evangelical university, which shall go unnamed, pulled off an impressive prank. It was a major event for the school, and the donors and board were present. The founding president had just finished giving a talk on the amazing accomplishments that his university had made for the kingdom of God when the students unfurled their plan—literally. A huge banner that had been concealed somehow behind a beam was let loose, and as it unrolled from the ceiling everyone present could read what it said: "Is this really the best God can do?"

I often think of that story when I see the church swell with pride at its achievements, or when I swell with pride over the great theology book I have published most recently. By contrast, when I am humbled by the complexity of the social and intellectual issues the church faces, I feel that I am in the right place. "My grace is sufficient for you, for my power is made perfect in weakness," is the message that Paul received. "So," he decided, "I will boast all the more gladly of my weaknesses, so that the power of Christ may dwell in me" (2 Cor. 12:9). And he adds, "For whenever I am weak, then I am strong" (v. 10).

It is my privilege to teach theology to men and women who have a call to ordained ministry in the church. On the opening day of their first class I try to shock students out of the expectation that theology is about boring business-as-usual. Opening the class—like opening this book—I wonder: How can I convince them that doing theology is not just about abstract doctrines and memorizing creeds from the past, that it's about the always challenging task of listening attentively to *all* the ways the Spirit of God speaks?

During a recent first class, an African American woman named Nicole spontaneously introduced a story that brilliantly brought this point home. As an intern in her evangelical church, she had been called to the hospital to be with a twenty-three-year-old woman during the last hours of her life. When Nicole came into the room, the young woman asked her own family to leave and then told Nicole, "I am not a Christian, and I do not want to be treated as a Christian. Not now, while I am dying, and not after I am dead. Please convince my family to let me be who I am!" Nicole then went out to the waiting room, where the family (one of the leading families in her church) begged her to pray with their daughter and to bring her to the Lord before it was too late.

Nicole told us, "I had no idea what to do. I have never prayed so hard in my entire life." For the next few hours, this young minister helped the dying girl and her family to make peace, to reconcile, to accept each other where they were, and to learn to love each other during the last moments of the young girl's life. No theology book ever written, no doctrine or teacher, could have given Nicole the wisdom in that hour to know what to say and do. "My grace is sufficient for you, for my power is made perfect in weakness." In theology, as in all of discipleship, when you are weak, then you are strong.

I suggest that Nicole's attitude is a model for the entire church. Ours is a revolutionary period, a time of transition, an era of new paradigms. Along with all other traditional American institutions, the church is struggling to respond to unprecedented challenges. If those of us in leadership are honest, we have to admit that we don't *really* know how to manage this change. We don't really know how to pastor a new kind of church or lead a denomination into the future or solve the problems of social injustice and global climate change. Most of us have a hard enough time just integrating our faith with the intricacies of our own day-to-day lives.

And yet, there are reasons for optimism. The most faithful and forward-looking responses to this changing world are not cynicism, egoism, or despair, and *the new paradigms do not require one to abandon all language of God*. Faith in Christ has not become irrelevant, and Jesus' message is not to be relegated to museums or the dustbins of history. Still, as a church we've got to do a much better job. In order to be effective, we will have to be lighter on our feet and much more adaptable and open to change than we have been so far. We need to accept a whole new assortment of best practices that are emerging outside of traditional church structures, and we need to bring them right into the heart of church and social ministries today. Never before have the stakes of complacency and inactivity been so high.

> *The church needs to be lighter on its feet and more adaptable to change.*

Some may wish they had been born into a more stable world, a world less fraught with such knotty challenges. But we must play the hand that we've been dealt. As Kenny Rogers says, we have to "know when to hold 'em, know when to fold 'em."[2] The question is how to discover concrete ways to play our game—which is an ultimately serious game—more effectively.

3. Why the Answers Must Be Theological (and What That Means)

Every Christian has a theology. For that matter, so does every Jew or Muslim or Hindu. A theology, in the broadest sense, just means what you believe about God (*theos*). Tragically, theology somehow got turned into a professional sport—a move that produced many of the negative tendencies that we already know from professional sports in America (except for the high salaries).

The invention of "theologians" as the professional authorities on Christian belief may turn out to be one of the really damaging things that have occurred in the history of the church. This invention doesn't get as much press as the invention of clergy—which has tended to undercut the "priesthood of all believers"—but it's right up there in importance. As long as there are professional theologians, those who *don't* carry this honorific title begin to assume that they can't do theology or aren't allowed to. The result was almost inevitable: intelligent, thinking people tend to sit in pews and wait for someone else to tell them what they should believe. If what they hear from the pulpit or from other sources of theological authority matches what they happen to believe, then they feel confirmed in their sense that they are right (and others must be wrong). If what the theological authorities are saying does *not* match what they believe, their recourse is to leave the church, convinced that they have no place there. Or, they may stay, but with a vague feeling of unsettledness or even guilt, worrying that their own religious intuitions and experiences don't quite fit in. Some become rebels, with no recourse but to protest against the church establishment from outside. Others just give up their own beliefs, bow to authority, and begin trying to believe what the professional theologians tell them they *ought* to believe.

None of these solutions is good. The professionalization of theology has taken it out of the hands (and heads) of those to whom it really belongs: every believing person, and every person who would like to believe. The results have been not only unproductive but also damaging for the spiritual lives of many who are Christians or who would like to know more about this Way.

Of course, churches have tried out a variety of means to address people's confusion about what they really believe. Some years ago, people began to define a sub-group of church-attendees as "seekers." Making room for seekers allows people to participate in the religious community as fully as they wish, yet without having to pretend that they believe things that they don't believe. I sometimes wish that whole churches would describe themselves as seekers—Christian communities where every attendee brings what he or she knows and has experienced of God, yet where no one claims to have God fully figured out. But there's also a downside to this term. Its very meaning contrasts "seekers" with "possessors." So it tends to imply that the rest of the people in the community already *have it*, whereas the seekers are the second-class citizens who are merely trying to *find it*. This then tends to create yet another two-tiered system, another version of the "haves" and the "have-nots." It's obvious such thinking doesn't fit for "a people on the Way." The real contrast is not seekers versus possessors, but seeking and finding—and seeking some more. Since the moments of finding, we believe, never occur without the participation of God, pride and possessiveness are not exactly the right responses.

So what's the first step in returning theology to the people?

A Theology Is a World-and-Life-View

The quickest way to understand why the dichotomy between professional theologians and the rest of us won't work is to talk about worldviews. A worldview is just what it sounds like: your overall view of the world, the cosmos, and everything in it. Until you think about it, much of your worldview is probably subconscious. *Others* can often describe what we really believe by watching how we live, but we may be unaware of it. Since worldviews also include many beliefs about how one should live, I prefer to call them *world-and-life-views*, or WLVs for short.

Every person has a WLV, a set of beliefs about what exists and what is most valuable. Some WLVs include beliefs about ultimate reality; some of *those* affirm that God is the ultimate reality; and some of *those* are Christian WLVs. So you see that a theology is only one kind of a WLV, and a Christian theology is only one form of theology. Jewish, Muslim, and Hindu practices all presuppose WLVs that are theological. Existentialism, materialism, and the "scientism" of a person like Richard Dawkins are non-theological WLVs. In the end, *every person who carries out conscious actions in the world possesses a WLV,* whether or not he or she is aware of it.

> Everyone who acts in the world has a world-view, conscious or not.

One of my early jobs was teaching philosophy in a university in California. My first semester I was assigned to teach four sections of Critical Thinking, and every semester after that for some years I taught one or two additional sections of that same class. You probably already know that classes like critical thinking and freshman comp are pretty far down the popularity charts. I didn't realize until I walked into the class the first day, however, that most students viewed my class as one of the most onerous requirements of their entire freshman year. I either had to find a way to make critical thinking fun, or my teaching career was quickly going to become hell on earth. Gradually I found a model that worked—so well, in fact, that teaching critical thinking became one of the great joys of my teaching career. The secret is WLVs. Every freshman student had to do what I'm now asking you to do. Each of them had to bring to awareness the beliefs, attitudes, and values that he or she held at the subconscious level. Concrete beliefs and values came first, since they're easier to access. Then gradually the students moved to more and more abstract beliefs and values. By the end of the class, students could identify their WLVs and show how these beliefs (implicitly or explicitly) guide their actions. For the final exam I gave them hard moral and ethical and political dilemmas, and they had to compose answers to them by appealing to their own WLV. The class became famous; students would say, "Yeah, for Clayton's final you have to write out your whole worldview!"

Implicitly, I was teaching that philosophy, like theology, is an amateur sport. Every human being who knows that he or she will someday die naturally engages in philosophy. Hence, I used to argue, there should be no such thing as a "professional philosopher." It was fascinating to explore with students what their WLVs really were and then to track the complex ways that their WLVs supported (or undercut) their actions. Now people under thirty may have an easier time surfacing what they really believe. But if they can do it, why can't every adult? Is it that we're afraid that what we really believe is not what our parents taught us or what our churches say we should believe—and perhaps not even what *we* thought we believed before we started thinking about the subject?

The same thing is true of theology. *Theology is just the shape your WLV takes if you believe in God.* For this reason, theology is—or at least *ought* to be—an amateur sport. Everyone who believes in God is, by that very fact, a theologian, and everyone who believes that God is somehow revealed in the one called Jesus Christ is, to that extent, a Christian theologian. If so many of us are theologians, then the idea of a "professional theologian" is a misnomer. It's a dangerous concept that can easily disenfranchise ordinary believers as they struggle to get clear on where they really stand.

> *Theology is just the shape your world-view takes if you believe in God.*

In fact, as we've already seen, the situation today is much worse. Professional theologians (whether they intend it or not) often end up training believers in what they are *supposed* to believe, producing the sorts of negative consequences I mentioned in the Introduction. I want to suggest a radically different model. If some people are to be paid for being theologians, then they should view themselves as coaches, not just as conveyers of true propositions. Just as a good soccer coach runs drills that help players develop skills and improve their game by building on their own strengths, so theologians should teach in such a way that helps believers get better at recognizing and formulating their own beliefs.

Of course, along the way there's content to learn as well. We must continue to teach what's in the Christian Scriptures, since they are the primary texts about Jesus. We also need to teach how these texts have been interpreted throughout history. But do we really need to be doctrinaire and exclusivist in how we do this? What if we start teaching what have been the core Christian questions and answers over the last 2000 years, and then asking the men and women in our classes to develop their own personal affirmations (testimonies) on the central topics of the Christian faith? I'll come back to this idea shortly and describe how this might be done.

Imagine letting theology classes be more like the Critical Thinking classes I used to teach. Future ministers might be asked to write out their Christian world-and-life view, to learn to debate openly (and well!) about what they believe, and then to become proficient at applying it to real-life situations in their lives, in congregations, and in the world today. Imagine how such training would change preaching and ministry and church leadership! Now imagine what would happen if local churches and other Christian groups started doing the same thing with *every person* who is trying to understand what it means to live life with a Christian WLV. Imagine groups of us struggling together to apply our Christian WLVs to the burning questions in our local communities and to the global challenges facing humanity—and then putting our conclusions and resolutions into action. A lot of honest and much-needed conversations would start to happen. And the results, I suggest, could well be revolutionary. That, in a nutshell, is the *transforming Christian theology* vision I hope you'll begin to share.

Sources for Christian World-and-Life-Views

It should be unnecessary to say, but treating theology as a WLV is not to demean it, to lower it in stature, or to rob it of all authority. Indeed, isn't the opposite true? I believe that a theology that's merely a list of propositions that one is supposed to believe is far *less* significant. Jesus said that the man or woman who wants to follow him must love his Way even more than his or her own life (Lk. 14:26). Once it's acknowledged that each of us has a WLV, we can start to ask questions about what role God really plays in this view. Christian discipleship is not about a bunch of oughts that you don't really believe; it's about the life-view by which you really live. As a result, theology as WLV requires a level of honesty from each person that a lot of Christians are just not used to bringing to their week-to-week church practices.

Some people have told me, "I don't need theology. Theology is abstract and overly intellectual. I just want to follow Jesus." If I thought the idea of WLVs replaced or distracted from following Jesus, I wouldn't put it forward; in fact, I wouldn't have written this book in the first place. But the assumption is wrong; there is no conflict *and can be no conflict* between the two. To follow Jesus well is going to take a bit of thought. Who is he? What were the key themes of his ministry? How do we speak and live those themes powerfully in today's context? How and where does God speak today? If you don't bring your underlying beliefs on these topics to the surface, how do you know how to live? Perhaps you're being guided by some faulty assumptions, such as, "I can have inner, infallible certainty of what is the right thing for the church as a whole to do if it's to be genuinely Christian," or "Except for my pastor, no one else has any knowledge, experience, or expertise that I need in order to follow Jesus well." We're often tempted to take a shortcut from our own inner feelings of conviction to action in the world. It's far wiser to let inner leadings be mediated through the broader sense of who God is and what we need—in short, through a WLV.

It's therefore crucial to pause for a moment and to ask: What are some of the important sources for doing theology as a world-and-life-view? Well, the sources for a given WLV will vary a bit depending on the view. The Bible is the primary formative source for a Christian WLV, just as the Qur'an is formative for Muslims and the Vedas and Upanishads are formative for Hindus. (Of course, not only religious people have formative texts; the books of Karl Marx play the major role for Marxists, and the works of Jean-Paul Sartre and Albert Camus are central for existentialists.) I like to use something called the Wesleyan Quadrilateral in describing the sources of theology: Scripture, tradition, experience, and reason.

Reason

Scripture   **How We Know God**   **Experience**

Tradition

Scripture

A Christian WLV is going to have a lot to do with Jesus, whether as symbol, moral exemplar, great prophet, living Lord, or all of the above. The central sources on the life and teachings of Jesus are the New Testament documents, which themselves grow out of the canonical texts of the Hebrew Bible. Thus these documents are going to be authoritative for Christians in one way or another. Exactly in what *way* they are authoritative has been a matter of deep disagreement among many Christians, and wars (certainly symbolic wars, and sometimes worse) have been and continue to be fought over this question. For Christians today, I suggest, the key thing is not to get your doctrine of Scripture exactly right before you start; rather, it is to use Scripture—deeply, intelligently, and constantly—as you seek to address the difficult questions of our day in your thoughts and actions.

Tradition

Because of my position, at least once a month some person sends me an essay or book in which he claims to have found the "true meaning" of the Scriptures. Invariably, these readings are completely individual and make no reference to the work that any scholar (or, for that matter, any other Christian) has ever done to interpret the scriptural texts. Apparently the authors believe that their intimate connection to the Holy Spirit is so flawless that no errors or prejudices could possibly creep in and mar their ability to hear what the Spirit is telling them about the texts. If you are like me, you greet such claims with a healthy dose of skepticism. Each of us is deeply enough influenced by his or her own presumptions, culture, historical period, and ego that we really need the corrective influence of others who are attempting to read the texts insightfully and accurately. This is the function of tradition. I do not view tradition as a compilation of infallible facts about the true meaning of the Bible to be accepted without question. Instead, I view it as the resource of many generations and many centuries of readers who have struggled with what God could be saying in and through the scriptural reports on the Hebrew tradition, on Jesus' life, and on the early church.

Experience

Experience is everyone's favorite source, and well it should be. If some-one tells you to believe something that conflicts totally with what you've experienced, sooner or later you're likely to abandon it. As we'll see later, experience is a great starting point for folks who are unsure exactly of their own WLV. However, we live in a culture and age where private, individual experience often trumps all other sources. Only honest judgment will reveal whether you are one who has not explored your own experience deeply enough to know what you really believe or one who has allowed private experience to overshadow the other sources.

Reason

The flip side of living in the "age of experience" is a suspicion of reason. In evangelical, progressive, and liberal churches today, reason is the most under-utilized of the four sources. Presentations of scientific results are rela-tively rare, despite the crucial role of science in our world today, and atten-tion to philosophical reflection comes infrequently if at all. Nor do those who have left the churches altogether—the seekers and those who are "spiritual but not religious"—manage in general to find a better balance between inner experience on the one side and careful reflection and study on the other. I am immensely encouraged, however, to see younger Christians, often in emerging churches and other non-traditional forms of Christian community, thinking very deeply about the core questions of their faith. Perhaps we are heading into an age when people will find it easier than in the late twentieth century to balance the four sources.

These four sources are not meant to be exclusive. Other theological sources are sometimes listed separately, including contemporary culture, sci-ence, other world religions, prayer, spiritual practices, and the experience of the oppressed. Although I think most of these can be fit into the preceding list, I agree that it's sometimes valuable to emphasize these other sources as well—as long as one doesn't ignore the primary four. The point is not to construct an exclusive list but to provide a sense of the areas you can turn to as you work to figure out your own WLV.

4. Postmodernity Makes Theologians of Us All

n part 3 we will look at the new social and cultural resources available to genuinely transformative theologies, including the new forms of social networking that led to the election of President Barack Obama. This radical morphing of the American public square won't go away because technologies never go backwards; they just keep building on top of one another. But in order to understand what these changes mean for the future of the church and what we're supposed to *do* with them, we must first place them into their broader cultural and historical context. *Postmodern* is the name scholars are using for this new context in which we find ourselves. Volumes have been written on the topic of postmodernity. But the basic idea is really not so complex. Since the distinction between "modern" and "postmodern" is basic to the newly emerging forms of religious believing and living, these two terms provide the best framework for interpreting what's happening around us.

 What Were the Assumptions of "Modernity"?

There's no question but that the advent of "modernity" was one of the most staggering transformations humanity has ever undergone—in fact, probably *the* most staggering transformation. Beginning in Western Europe and gradually spreading across the entire planet, the increasing technological abilities of the human race—the printing press, ships and navigation, city building, scientific knowledge, the construction of massive social and political systems, just to name a few—transformed every dimension of our existence. Indeed, by the end of the twentieth century human technological prowess had transformed the planet as a whole; today there is virtually no part of the earth, the oceans, or the atmosphere that does not bear the mark of Man.

Not surprisingly, all these changes encouraged a new world-and-life-view (WLV), which is to say, new ways of thinking about the world and our place in it. This new worldview has a certain coherence to it; one really can identify a distinctively modern worldview. Consider these three features. First, because human reason played the driving role in the scientific revolution, it's not surprising that *the powers of human reason* stand at the center of the picture. Reason, the Moderns taught us, brings "Enlightenment." By contrast, the things that don't directly contribute to scientific reason tended to be dismissed as part of the "dark ages" of humanity. For most of the modern period, for example, God, emotions, and women were unfortunately placed in the latter category.

Second, modernity was characterized by what scholars call *melioristic optimism*. The Moderns assumed that things would get better and better as humanity began to use its distinctive gift of reason to address, one by one, each of the social and political problems that it faced. Human potential was viewed as unlimited; hence, they assumed, it would only be a matter of time before humanity brings about the perfect, or virtually perfect, form of social organization—a sort of heaven on earth.

Third and finally, the Moderns tended to get stuck on an *either/or choice between absolutism and relativism*. You can see this false dilemma reflected in the two dominant theories of religion from the modern period. One model tacitly assumed (and modern philosophers often argued) that the dominant religious beliefs of Western Europe—Protestant and Roman Catholic Christianity—were the highest forms of religion, the only ones consistent with a genuinely enlightened mentality; one religion was the best and all others were inferior. The other major model of religion arose with the deists of the seventeenth century. This model suggested that all the differences between religions were only relative. Religions were concerned with matters of taste, acculturation, or upbringing, not matters of ultimate truth. Hence the enlightened individual would rise above all such distinctions and not treat them as significant. As a result, many of the Enlightenment's figures advocated a pure "religion of reason" that did away with the primitive beliefs, doctrines, and practices of the traditional religions. Reason determined one's most important choices; all the rest was relative.

In my view, the dominance of modern ideals was *not* a good thing for the church. Moving away from pure reason as primary authority, melioristic optimism, and the either/or of absolutism and relativism is beginning to free Christians from some fixations we never should have had. It's also opening some exciting doors, as we'll see in a minute. But even if you happen to be a lover of modernity, the descriptive fact remains the same: our culture as a whole is shifting in a new direction.

In many ways Protestantism as we have known it (and as it is institutionalized in our current church structures) should be seen as the quintessentially modern religion. It was born out of the same turn to subjective certainty based on inner experience that made Descartes the father of modern philosophy. It produced comprehensive, systematic theologies that rivaled the great philosophical systems of high modernity. In what came to be known as "cultural Protestantism," it supported the superiority of European culture. As such, it was complicit in the many negative consequences Eurocentrism had around the globe in the modern period: racism, colonialism, xenophobia, even genocide. Among these painful consequences was an unbridled capitalism that scholars have repeatedly linked to Protestant theology and that justified (and continues to justify) policies of global injustice on the part of Europeans and North Americans.

In this and many other ways, modern Protestantism supported a thinking preoccupied with centers and margins—with itself, of course, always at the center. You find the same patterns of center and margins whether you look at church architecture, doctrines of Scripture, church liturgies, the central role of the pastor, or even modern theories of world missions. It is thus not surprising, as our culture transitions from modern to postmodern, that Protestantism should be in particular trouble.

One side effect of this new, modern worldview was a rethinking of the centuries of human history that had preceded it. If we enlightened ones are now modern, then all who came before us must have been *pre*modern. Thus the Moderns invented the narrative that the Greeks had enjoyed a purely rational form of art and society; that the Christian church had gradually undercut that culture of reason; and that the medieval period (the nearly 1,000 years from the fall of Rome in the early fifth century until the advent of modernity) had been nothing but "the dark ages." This modern narrative implied that any talk of religious belief, God, divine action, or revelation was a throwback to the Dark Ages and should be left behind as quickly as possible.

Transition to a Postmodern World

René Descartes (1596–1650) is often called "the father of modern philoso-phy," and the modern period is often said to have started around the year 1600. (Other scholars have shown, however, that its roots go back to at least 200 years earlier, and maybe more.[1]) Like all major cultural phenomena, modernity has no precise beginning or end, no perfect definition in terms of necessary and sufficient conditions. Despite what you may have read in textbooks, there is no "essence" of modernity. Large movements like the modern period, together with the worldviews that accompany them, need to be understood more in terms of "fuzzy set theory." Big cultural movements can be described approximately and for the most part, but they cannot be captured by a definition. They are like a major river flooding its banks, or even like a tsunami: they do not follow precise channels and are thus very hard to describe. Still, the fuzziness of these huge movements in no way undercuts the power of their world-and-life-views over those who are car-ried along by their currents.

Thus it will not surprise you that scholars hold heated debates about whether modernity has ended, whether we are now in a "postmodern" period, or whether we are still the children of "late modernity." (My men-tor at Yale, Louis Dupré, was a major participant in these debates, and I recommend his work for people who want to go deeper.) Here I will only argue, without all the technicalities, that the changes we are seeing around us today represent such a radical departure from the worldview of moder-nity that they require us to speak of the dawning of a *postmodern* era. Let's consider, very briefly, the key features of this postmodern era, before turning to the more urgent question: What does it mean to believe and act as follow-ers of Jesus Christ in this radically new cultural setting? There are exciting new possibilities that are opening up for us. Before we can embrace them, though, we must understand them.

There are various ways to define postmodernism. Some define it in terms of the demise of all stable structures of knowledge and reference (post-structuralists like Jacques Derrida).[2] Others define it in terms of the demise of all "meta-narratives" (Jean-François Lyotard). Still others speak of the emergence of a new global consciousness, based on the knowledge of our common origin, one that transcends the modern worldview. Here you might think of Brian Swimme and Thomas Berry's brilliant *The Universe Story* (HarperSanFrancisco, 1994), or the "all quadrants, all levels" worldview of Ken Wilber. But you might also think, more simply, of the common environmental crisis now faced by all life on this planet, which will either unite us all into unified action or result in the death of millions of people and the loss of many or most of the species on earth.[3] In fact, *all* of the factors just mentioned are part of the global change of consciousness that humanity is now undergoing, which we call postmodernism. In *The Future of Christology*, for example, the theologian Roger Haight speaks of the four parts of postmodern consciousness: radical historical consciousness, critical social consciousness, pluralist consciousness, and a cosmic consciousness.[4]

However we define our new postmodern age, it's clear that it means a break, and perhaps a radical one, from each of the features of modernity that I described above. Thus we find that postmodern Christians are not particularly interested in exact lists of doctrines. They do not think that there is a universal right answer for how Christians should act in all cultural situations and at all times. They *do* go back again and again to the life and teachings of Jesus, since these continue to be the model for Christian practice and belief. But they do so with a fuller sense of how complex discipleship has now become. They are aware of the nuances of interpretation and the ubiquitous role of changing situations and settings as they struggle to determine what it means to live in a "Christ-like" manner. Compared to their predecessors, they are pragmatic idealists. They want their faith to make a difference in the world, but they also know that the process will have to be interactive and dialogical, that they can't start with ready-made doctrinal systems and deduce all further steps from there. They are clear on wanting to be followers of Jesus' Way.

It's not hard to say in general terms what discipleship means; it means, *in this new situation, here and now, to participate in God's bringing about the kingdom of God in ways that reflect Jesus' transformative responses to the situations he encountered in his ministry.* But postmodern Christians know that it takes some interpretive work—what people call "hermeneutics"—to say what a Jesus-like

> *Disciples reflect Jesus' transformative responses to the situations he encountered in his ministry.*

identity is and what actions it entails. The call (and the costs) of being a disciple may be constant, but the actual living of discipleship must be ever responsive to a constantly changing world.

The postmodern shift has clear implications for the church. For each of the three characteristics of modernity—the authority of reason, the optimism of "things will just get better and better," and the dichotomy between absolutism and relativism—there is corresponding postmodern tendency. *The three central features of postmodern religion are the focus on practice, the turn to a more pragmatic idealism, and the stress on deep, life-changing convictions in a world of rampant religious plurality.*

With the old model, reason had to lay out the path first, and then you could walk it. Today, people start out with a general sense of what they believe and clarify the details as they go. Specific beliefs walk hand in hand with practice; indeed, they're often subsequent to practice and experience. Detailed views of Scripture, God, and Christ (just to mention a few) are more like on-the-job training. You get hired first and join the firm, and you assume that you can work the rest out as you go along.

For most people today, the old optimism is long gone. Younger people haven't given up their hopefulness (despite what the older generation often says), but it's a sober optimism, one that seems to have matured earlier than in the last few generations. Many cultural observers are calling it pragmatic idealism. It's an attitude that seems to say, "With God's help, we can do some powerful and transformative things here. But it's going to require some time, some big partnerships, and some willingness to compromise and meet people halfway. What we achieve won't look exactly like our dreams; lots of stuff is going to change along the way. But let's set our sights high and be part of something bigger than ourselves, something with enduring value."

With the old model, the moment your foundations became at all uncertain, relativism would rear its ugly face. Only a very high view of Scripture, for example, could save us from the slippery slope leading into the dreaded depths of atheism, nihilism, and despair. Placing so much weight on the foundations led to some pretty harsh judgments on other religions, and even harsher judgments on Christians who were "soft" on Scripture. I witnessed the inquisition that followed the publication of Harold Lindsell's *The Battle for the Bible* in 1976, and I can tell you, it was not pretty. It was Christian modernity at its worst.

Today's postmodern believers hold Christian convictions that are no less deep and life-changing, and they are guided by Scripture no less thoroughly than the foundationalists were. But the either/or logic is gone. The "I'm right, you're wrong" has been replaced by something closer to "I believe this is true and right, and I'm ready to talk with you about my convictions. But in this world of radical religious pluralism I also encounter people with very different convictions. I leave their fate to God. My faith is not lessened by the existence of deep differences of belief."

5. Postmodern Believing

O utside of the world of conservative evangelicals, many American Christians seem to have some pretty serious problems saying what it is that they believe with all their heart, soul, strength, and mind. We act as though we're really unsure what sorts of things (outside of science and common sense) we're allowed to have deep, life-changing beliefs about—beliefs that we take seriously as probably true. Why has believing become so hard?

Three Last Gasps of Late Modernity

1. Scientism

"Scientism" still dominates the academic world and many segments of our society. Scientism is the belief (dogma) that, in a science-dominated world, one should only have beliefs about matters that have been empirically settled. We can believe that the speed of light is 299,792,458 meters per second, or that light is both wave and particle. But when it comes to things like a sunset, the beauty of the world, or the sense that life is valuable or meaningful, we are only supposed to have *experiences*. After all, we are told, these are not the sorts of things that anyone *can* hold true or false beliefs about—with the exception, again, of the scientific, empirically accessible aspects of experience. Regarding the great questions that humanity has continually posed to itself—the questions with which philosophers have wrestled and on which religious persons have differed—one is supposed to say, "We will just never know." One then presumably returns to her everyday life and pours her energies into things that matter more, where she can "really make a difference" in the world.

2. Return to the Pre-modern

Scientism is one late modern answer to the question of what we may believe. It still dominates in Europe and North America, as it does in much of Japan and China. The next answer is just as unattractive. This one thumbs its nose at the entire modern worldview and returns to what is essentially a premodern mindset. *All* the modern concern with religious plurality, and all attempts to integrate one's faith with developments in modern science and philosophy, are left by the wayside. Moving back to a pre-modern worldview, we are told, is the only way to preserve all the claims of Scripture, and hence the only way to be authentically Christian in today's world. The irony should be obvious: these people retain authenticity precisely by *not* engaging with today's world, substituting a first-century context for a twenty-first-century one. Of course it's easy to be a Christian if you adjust your beliefs about history, science, and culture to first-century standards. But it's hardly an incarnational approach, since it doesn't engage the world that actually surrounds us.

3. Fundamentalism

Fundamentalism in religion represents the last gasp of religion in the *modern* context. Religion, conceived under the modern paradigm, always fights to define its exact boundaries. Thus modern religion, at least in its most extreme forms, attempts to exactly specify the propositions that it affirms. Exact boundaries can be drawn, for example, by arguing that the Bible is dictated by God (the "plenary" doctrine of inspiration) and thus is utterly without error, including in all matters of history and science. The doctrine that the Qur'an was literally dictated by Allah makes the same claim. Or one can try to delineate a complete list of the central Christian propositions, as Carl F. H. Henry[1] attempted to do in his theology, and as the authors of the list of "Christian fundamentals" did in the 1880s. From there, in classical modern fashion, one then deduces exactly what are the ethical demands of Christianity. Moderns like this. It allows them to know, *independent of all cultural or historical contexts* (including the contextual leading of the Holy Spirit, I fear), exactly what is *the* Christian thing to do in any given situation. Many modern theologians have then fought tooth and nail to defend their list of true propositions from scientists, philosophers, and advocates of other religious traditions.

Perhaps these three strategies sound familiar to you. What's encouraging is that they set the stage for some much-needed new ways of believing. Postmodern believing is not less deep and powerful than modern believing. But it encourages some very different (and, I think, refreshing) attitudes toward certainty and doubt.

Doubt Is Not Sin

Soon after my conversion I was asked to be a "counselor" at a Billy Graham Crusade. I served in this role many times, which I suppose means that I have "won many people for Christ." The biggest crusade I participated in took place in a large sports stadium. When the evangelist called for people to convert to Christ and the organ started to play "Just as I Am, without One Plea," counselors like me would gradually stand up all over the stadium and make our way to the altar that had been set up in front. (They never told us this, but obviously this huge group of people that was popping up all over and walking to the altar would give the audience the impression that about a third of the people who had come to the meeting were converting to Christ. You'd almost feel left out if you *didn't* go forward!) We could all recognize each other by a particular sign, so we could tell who had actually come forward to get converted, and we each picked a convert to counsel by standing on his or her right side. After we explained Billy Graham's Four Spiritual Laws to our convert-candidates, we prayed the Sinner's Prayer with them, and they were saved. We had to make sure that they were safe from any doubts that Satan might bring to them the next day (like, "Was that for real?"). So we would have them memorize a simple jingle to help them hold out against the devil's temptations. It went: "God says it in His Word. I believe it in my heart. That settles it forever."

The trouble is, not only for new converts but also for a very large number of committed Christians and seekers, that *doesn't* settle it forever. Each of us encounters some doctrines, or some points in our lives, where believing is not quite so easy, where the doubts refuse to depart. Some questions and concerns are relatively trivial, and some remain amorphous, but a few are much more serious and much more precise. As an example of the first, relatively trivial kind, I well remember being a teenager and thinking, "I know every word in the Bible is supposed to be true. But somehow I just have trouble believing that women should have to cover their heads in church 'because of the angels' (1 Cor. 11:10)." Apparently (according to some scholars) Paul thought that if the women in church left their heads uncovered and the angels saw their long hair, it would cause the angels to lust, that is, feel sexual attraction toward them. "Are angels really the kind of beings that struggle with lust when they see a woman's long hair in church?" I wondered. Paul's main reason was different: "A man ought not to have his head veiled, since he is the image and reflection of God; but woman is the reflection of man" (v. 7). I didn't find this reason convincing either. I discovered, however, that my conservative friends and pastors didn't appreciate questions like these.

Other doubts reflect more fundamental concerns. Some of these are profound, such as the lifelong struggle with the problem of evil and suffering. A few years ago a woman sat in my office and described how her sister had slowly and painfully died of bone cancer. She had big doubts: "Let's suppose that God can and does answer our little prayers, like helping us find a date or a parking spot. If God is able to do supernatural things like that at any time, then why did he do nothing while my sister slowly died? He must have had some particular reason to make her suffer and die like this. But what could that reason have been? Was she somehow more wicked than the people who *don't* die of cancer?" In the end, she told me, "After watching what my sister went through, I just can't believe in this God anymore."

 ## Return to a Thinking Faith

Often, the way the debate is set up confronts thinking Christians (and non-Christians also) with an impossible choice. Those on our right seem to be saying, "Believe, or shut up," while those on our left argue, "*All* religious believing is absurd. Humans just can't know anything about matters of ultimate reality or ultimate value." According to them, religious belief only leads to dissent, to distraction, and ultimately to religious wars and fundamentalism. It's better simply to trash the whole thing, or at best, allow religion to add a little warm, pastel coloring to the admittedly rather cold and indifferent universe that science offers us. "Still," they add, "it's fine if you want to send your kids to Sunday school (or have them bar or bat mitzvahed, if you're Jewish), since a little exposure to religion might help make them more moral people. Just don't let them take the stuff too seriously." Many in our society today experience this dichotomy as a complete stalemate. Both sides are unattractive, we feel. And yet we wonder whether there can even be a third option.

I believe that this dichotomy is simply false. There *is* a third option. In fact, a whole rich world of options lies between scientific reductionism on the one hand and an uncompromising belief-without-doubts on the other. Two relatively minor adjustments open up this space for postmodern believing. One of them involves reordering believing and belonging; I return to it in the next section. The other involves giving up the assumption that doubts should be viewed as sin. Having questions about inherited beliefs is not a sign of a willful spirit, spiritual immaturity, or moral turpitude. It is simply the way that mature human minds work as they struggle to integrate the various facets of their experience into a coherent whole.

This is such a simple step, and yet it is at the same time immensely liberating. Many of us have unconsciously imbibed the principle that doubting always means sinning, without ever realizing what we have swallowed. I remember gradually recognizing this fact after reading Gary Gutting's book, *Religious Belief and Religious Scepticism*. There Gutting affirms that religious belief requires "a total commitment to its implications for action that is incompatible with continuing reflection on its truth."[2] According to Gutting, it is "simply foolish" to "[give] up everything for a belief that I think requires further discussion and evaluation."[3] But I'm just not convinced that the commitment needed for action is incompatible with continuing reflection. Why can't I continue to be a disciple of Jesus in my actions, while sometimes encountering doubts in my thought? Can't I be faithful to Jesus' Way even while I am struggling with many of the doctrinal claims from within the theological tradition? Here I would prefer to follow Søren Kierkegaard, who in *Concluding Unscientific Postscript* quotes Lessing:

> Thesis 4: Lessing said: If God were holding complete truth in his right hand and in his left a singular and always restless striving after truth, a striving in which I would err for ever and a day, and if he directed me to choose between them,
>
> I would humbly ask for his left hand and say, Father, grant me this, for pure truth belongs to you alone.[4]

The amazing thing about allowing ourselves to acknowledge doubts, I have found, is that over the long haul it does not *increase* doubting but actually helps to *decrease* its frequency and severity. It's like other areas in life: when we attempt to sweep things under the table or hide them in the closet, they somehow start festering; their influence increases and gradually they begin to dominate in a very negative fashion. They just won't stay hidden. By contrast, when we bring our fears out into the open and examine them by the light of day, we often find that they are rather less intractable. After all, during the light of day we can consult with friends, teachers, and pastors; we can read books on the subject; and we can bring the whole powers of our own mature reflection to bear on the problems. When we're in the closet, we just can't see clearly enough to do these things!

If we are allowed to bring the full range of our adult problem-solving capacities to bear on our doubts, we can often find some constructive ways through our difficulties. After all, many of the questions that people ask us, and that we ask ourselves, involve serious issues that deserve careful attention. The net result is often that we can distinguish then what lies at the heart of our own religious life from the issues that lie more at the periphery, with the result that the doubting becomes less destructive that we had thought. One result of responding in this way is that we become much more able to listen to the doubts of others and to respond intelligently to their questions than we would have before.

 ## Belonging, Behaving, Believing

That brings me to the second major feature of postmodern believing. I first learned this from Phyllis Tickle's fantastic book, *The Great Emergence* (Baker, 2008), but it is now so widely cited on the Web that most people have forgotten where it comes from. Like many other people, I was taught that the only route to being a disciple of Jesus—and indeed, the only route to *any* serious Christian identity—was *believe, behave, belong*. Many of us have been told from the very beginning to build our lives around the verse, "If you confess with your mouth, 'Jesus is Lord,' and believe in your heart that God raised him from the dead, you will be saved" (Rom. 10:9, NIV). So we first sit down and try to *believe* the Christian propositions that people tell us we should believe. (In more conservative Christian circles, this means that you have to believe that Scripture is the inerrant Word of God. Once you believe that, you are committed to believing a very large number of propositions indeed!) Then we try to *behave* in line with all these propositions. Generally we are told that obedience is always "by the grace of God." Still, we know that if we mess up, it sure isn't *God's* fault! Finally, only when things are going well with the believing and behaving can we really *belong*, that is, be a member of the Christian community in good standing. When things aren't going that well, we feel that we really shouldn't be there.

Like many others, I have found these marching orders to be the cause of rather continuous guilt. We know that we want to live the "Spirit-filled life"; we want to "live by grace" and to enjoy a "victorious Christian walk with God." But then we encounter some rather steep demands among the items on the list of what we're supposed to believe and do. I, for one, kept stumbling over the phrase in the Sermon on the Mount, "Be perfect, therefore, as your heavenly Father is perfect" (Matt. 5:48). You've got to admit that sets a pretty high standard for the *believe, behave, belong* game. When, for whatever reason, we begin to worry that we aren't quite living up to the standard, we start to ask whether we really belong in the body of God's Chosen. If they let us in at all, we'd better seat ourselves in the very back row of the church, preserving the forward rows for the holier members of the congregation. (Indeed, some of us fear that the Moral Patrol may show up at any instant to remove us from the sanctuary, since we don't really belong there in the first place!)

A postmodern understanding of religious believing in general, and of Christian discipleship in particular, reverses the order. I don't perfectly understand all the details of Jesus' Way, and I *know* that I don't perfectly follow what I do understand. But for cultural, historical, and personal reasons, it is the way that I have seen God. There is no other way that is a live option for me, and dispensing with the attempt to seek and to know God through Christ is somehow just not a live option. As Simon Peter said to Jesus at one point, more in perplexity than as a resounding statement of faith, "Lord, to whom [else] can we go? You have the words of eternal life" (Jn. 6:68). One can even repeat those words in times of despair. As Martin Luther said, perhaps also with more perplexity than bravado, "Here I stand; I can do no other. God help me. Amen!"[5]

And here is the liberating insight: in that I find myself on this Way, *I already belong.* I may not be certain about many of the beliefs, and I may find myself continually falling short. I may have troubles with the institutional church. But I can't help belonging to that group of people who are associated with this Way, just as I belong to the One who somehow first found me. The life given through grace by One who transcends me is not driven by the motor of my believing; its fuel is not the quality of my behaving. Nor is it primarily about the particular denominational membership that I may use to identify myself. With all our warts and uncertainties, some of us just find ourselves with an attraction to this figure Jesus, or with powerful religious experiences associated with him, or with moral and political convictions in which his teachings play an

> *In that I find myself on Jesus' Way, I* already *belong.*

irreducible role. That belonging comes first. We want to be his disciples. It doesn't matter that we doubt, wander, wonder, and frequently knit our brows in confusion and despair. We are where we are. Perhaps we, like Martin Luther, can "do no other."

Years ago, a wise Presbyterian pastor named Blair Moffett tried to convince me of this point. I was a graduate student in religion and philosophy at Yale University and struggling with doubts. I told him I wasn't sure I could become a member of his church, because I wasn't sure that I could really affirm all the sentences new members were supposed to say out loud when they joined. It makes me smile to think of it now, but I even wrote out detailed philosophical critiques of those few short sentences in the Presbyterian hymnal. Blair tried to convince me that it wasn't about getting all the details right up front. We join others who find themselves on the Way, and then, as we walk together, we struggle to clarify our beliefs and to get clearer on our calling and on the nature of the One who calls us. In the end, as it turned out, Blair was right.

 ## Always Already on the Way

I don't think this point really sunk in for me until some years later, when I found myself standing in front of a large group of young Muslim students in Yogyakarta. I had traveled to Indonesia to speak to an interfaith conference. On the second afternoon I was to be "the Christian speaker" who, along with two Muslims and a Jew, would address the topic of the nature of the human person. As one would expect from any good young theology professor, I had carefully researched my topic and had prepared a brainy and rather abstract talk on the major tenets of Christian theological anthropology. But as I looked out over the faces of the 300 eager and intelligent Muslim students, it finally dawned on me. Whatever doubts and worries I might have about my own believing and behaving (and I had many), however problematic "Christian identity" might seem to me, in their young eyes I was indisputably a representative of Christianity. Suddenly I realized that the niceties didn't really matter. They knew me as one of the followers of Jesus, whom people call "Christians," and they would judge me in that light. I also knew that I wanted to be numbered among his followers. It would be downright dishonest to duck out of this role into some safe place of neutrality and agnosticism in order to nurse my philosophical worries.

At that moment I finally got it: the belonging, the identification with Jesus' Way, comes first, not last. Many of us realize that we are somehow *already there* as soon as we stop to think about it. "Here I am; I can do no other." We know the behaving matters, but it doesn't come first; it's not the precondition for belonging. I belong because of grace. Grace is *immer schon da*, as the German theologians say—it's "always already there."

The concern with behaving always comes second. I knew I had to try to act in a Jesus-like way with this group of impressionable young students; the details of my believing would have to sort themselves out later. (Or not.) For the moment, my task was to offer a more positive portrait of a Jesus-follower than they had encountered before. My Christian predecessors had done horrendous things to Muslims over centuries and centuries of our common history. The first step of behaving, I suddenly knew, was to admit how wrong these crusades were from the standpoint of the Jesus-Way. I threw away my prepared text and stepped up to the microphone to express my sorrow over what *we Christian believers* had done, and continue to do, to Muslim believers. As one identified with this Way, I had to start my talk on human nature by acknowledging *our* wrongs and expressing my sorrow about them.

That, in short, is the lesson of postmodern Jesus-discipleship: *belong, behave, believe*. It's not as neat and pretty as the account I was taught when young: "get your beliefs right, then get your life in order, and then you can join us." But then again, human existence is rarely as black and white, as neat and pretty, as we were taught when we were young.

6. "Everything Must Change"

E verything must change." These three words compose the title of a recent (and extremely important) work by Brian McLaren. In it he explains his motivation for writing the book:

> As a follower of God in the way of Jesus, I've been involved in a profoundly interesting and enjoyable conversation for the last ten years or so. It's a conversation about what it means to be "a new kind of Christian"—not an angry and reactionary fundamentalist, not a stuffy traditionalist, not a blasé nominalist, not a wishy-washy liberal, not a New Agey religious hipster, not a crusading religious imperialist, and not an overly enthused Bible-waving fanatic—but something fresh and authentic and challenging and adventurous.[1]

These new conversations are happening all around us today. They are crucial because the world is changing rapidly and radically. If we're going to speak and live Jesus' message in a relevant and powerful fashion, we have to find new ways of going about it. Many of the Christian structures we've inherited from past generations aren't up to the task. Brian is right:

> The versions of Christianity we inherited are largely flattened, watered down, tamed . . . offering us a ticket to heaven after death, but not challenging us to address the issues that threaten life on earth. Together we've begun to seek a fresh understanding of what Christianity is for, what a church can be and do, and most exciting, we're finding out that a lot of what we need most is already hidden in a trunk in the attic. Which is good news.[2]

The trouble is, humans don't love radical change. We learn a few things we're good at; we develop our (more or less effective) coping mechanisms; we form our basic beliefs and values; and then we want to spend the rest of our lives doing what we know—being with friends and family, enjoying life, and, if possible, doing some good while we're here. Just ask one of your friends who has lost a job or has been forced by the recent recession into a mid-life career change. Change may have its "up" side, but a lot of the *process* of changing can be pretty unpleasant.

Of course, it's never completely true that *everything* changes. No matter how great the external changes, we usually remain much the same person we were in the past, at least in our essential features. Societies and countries, as much as they may change, likewise usually retain many of their primary features. And through it all God remains God; God's essential nature remains unchanged.

But you have to admit, pretty much everything else nowadays is up for grabs. We are in the midst of the most rapid social and technological change that our species has ever undergone. When you look at predictions for the future, the curves that describe the rate of change just keep getting steeper and steeper. Take just one example: When the Iranian people took to the streets in the summer of 2009 to protest what appeared to be a rigged election, the leaders of the protest movement used SMS and Twitter to help get tens of thousands of people to coordinate their movements. The reliance on Twitter was so great at the high point of the protest marches that a State Department official emailed the CEO of Twitter.com and urgently requested that he not to take the system offline for routine maintenance, not even for an hour. Apparently the U.S. government felt that the future of Iran, and thus of the Middle East, turned on a social messaging website that didn't even exist a few years ago. The new media gave voices to people who would have been easily silenced in any previous world.

That is rapid change. Are churches as aware as the State Department was of the powerful roles now played by new structures, new technologies, and new ways of communicating? Are church leaders utilizing these new technologies to support their outreach and ministries? Do they even know what they are? As one of my young friends, Tripp Fuller, puts it, "Not to know the new media is not to exist in the world more and more people exist in." I encourage anyone over forty who thinks the world *hasn't* changed to spend an hour carefully interviewing a couple of people under eighteen about their technology use. Just one datum (you still need to do the interview): News.cnet.com recently reported that "the surge in text messaging is being driven by teens 13 to 17 years old, who on average send and receive about 1,742 text messages a month."[3] If you do the math, that's about fifty-eight text messages a day! This is just *not* the same world for which our present church communities were designed.

Parallels with the Fall of Rome

The church on earth is not immune to change. In fact, the church is now in a period of revolutionary cultural change very similar to the one St. Augustine faced when he penned that Christian classic, *The City of God.* Augustine was a classically educated scholar and the bishop of Hippo in northern Africa. He was also the inheritor of some 500 years of the Roman Empire, which extended throughout what was thought of as the civilized world. So Augustine and his age knew something of social stability and of the institutions it had spawned.

Indeed, the parallels are even stronger. Rome was the center of Augustine's empire, just as Europe and the United States have viewed themselves as the center and pinnacle of the modern civilized world. Europe literally colonized much of the planet, just as the Romans did. (Indeed "to colonize" comes from the Latin *colonia*, or "settled land," meaning any Roman settlement outside Italy.) The French controlled much of Africa; the British "Indian Empire" or *Raj* encompassed all of present-day India and Pakistan and more; and the United States was still engaging in CIA operations to make and break nation states according to U.S. interests well into the 1950s (and, many would say, well beyond). The Romans believed they had brought civilization to large portions of the "barbaric" world, which is also what modern European Christians believed. Ultimately, the colonized peoples rebelled against Roman control for political, economic, and religious reasons—just as the peoples of Asia and Africa rose up against Western rule in the last fifty years or so and demanded their independence. Still, old mentalities die hard.

In 410 C.E., at the peak of Augustine's career, the marauding "barbarians" from north of the Alps—the Visigoths—marched into Rome, the capital of the Empire, and sacked the city for three days. The attacks of September 11, 2001, pale in comparison. To Romans and Christians of that day it was unthinkable that uncivilized tribes should have their way with Rome. How could God allow it? As it turned out, the sacking of Rome was a major step toward the eventual fall of the Roman Empire.

For St. Augustine and his fellow believers, the world would never be the same again. From then on the church had to learn to survive in a radically different world than it had known up to that time. Against the standard human tendency to assume the future will always be like the past, Augustine set to work to figure out what would have to change, from core theologies to church structures to interpretations of discipleship. For some thirteen years (roughly 413–426 C.E.) he struggled to work out new conceptions of church, of being a Christian, and even of God's entire relationship with human history. He learned to distinguish things that we have perhaps not yet learned to separate: what belongs to "the city of man" and what really belongs to "the city of God" or "the eternal city."

 ## Changes in the Structure of Congregations

The situation we face today is not that different from the situation in Augustine's day. Structures that we took for granted, that we assumed were God-given—*structures to which we did not even imagine there could be alternatives*—are now collapsing around us. Mainline churches are simply not attracting significant proportions of the younger population in America, and there are no signs that this pattern is about to change. If for some reason all the persons in mainline churches today who are over the age of sixty-five were to disappear, *two thirds* of current church attendees would be gone. At some point age will remove the people who are currently carrying the main burden of keeping the mainline churches running and who are their most faithful attendees. There are no signs that younger people are about to flood into these same churches to replace the older generation when it departs. I need to say that again, in case you missed it: just because in the *past* younger people filled the churches as older people departed doesn't mean that it will happen again. *It really is possible that the next generation will not return to the old churches.* In fact, all the signs suggest that this is exactly what's happening now.

> It really is possible that the next generation will not return to the old churches.

At the second Transforming Theology conference we discussed this issue with heads and leaders of the mainline denominations. One of the participants described the situation brilliantly. He pointed out that the basic structure of congregations as we now know them was formed during the colonial period of American history and during the frontier period, when Europeans were moving westward across the American continent. During these centuries Christian congregations were among the primary organizing structures of American life. It wasn't too much, even in a small town, to have every major denomination represented by at least one congregation. Since the 1950s, however, technology and other cultural transformations have massively changed the structures of our society. The functions that congregations once served are being fulfilled in very different ways today. Huge numbers of these congregations are therefore no longer financially viable, and many of them teeter on the edge of collapse. One denominational leader described hundreds of congregations in a single rural region that are not going to make it, and a bishop from another denomination said that of the 400 churches under his charge, 200 of them were struggling for survival.

 ## Changes in the Structure of Denominations

The same is true of denominational structures. Today's denominations arose out of disputes that were of great importance to the people of past eras. Some disputes were theological, such as advocating or denying predestination; some surrounded powerful and charismatic figures, such as John Wesley, the founder of Methodism; and some concerned church practices, such as whether or not musical instruments should be allowed into worship services (and, if so, are only organs allowed, or can you let in violins as well?).

The truth is, the disputes that birthed many of today's denominations are no longer relevant by and large to the vast number of church attendees—and definitely not to folks outside the churches! There is simply not much "brand loyalty" left today for the denominations in America, and what there is of it decreases very sharply as you descend the age scale from seventy to twenty years old. For most people, mainline churches are interchangeable. Individuals and families will switch from one to another based on location or building, quality of the preaching, size of the youth program, or how many friends or acquaintances one has in a particular congregation. Again, for the growing number of folks who no longer feel comfortable in traditional churches, denominational labels matter even less.

Worse than that, the existing denominations are being weakened by sharp disputes that threaten to rend them asunder—and in some cases are already doing so. The question of homosexuality, and in particular the debate concerning the ordination of gay clergy, is the big "hot button issue" for church bodies today. In the public's eyes, it now overshadows the more traditional distinguishing features of the various denominations. Conservatives are threatening to bring about huge schisms in the major denominations around this issue alone, and in the Episcopal Church of America the schism is already occurring. Interestingly, the new alliances on the issue of gay ordination often cut *across* denominations, rather than along standard denominational lines. Some people are saying that the debate about gay clergy is the beginning of the end for many of the mainline denominations as we have known them.

But large structures like denominations do not pass away quickly. Many of them are likely still to be in existence for decades, even a century from now. The question concerns their social role: In the future will they be shapers of American society, or, like other Christian organizations from the past such as the Epworth League, will they exist only on the margins of this emerging new world?

The answer is not yet clear. In some cases, exciting experiments are underway right at the heart of existing structures. Think of Orthodox churches such as the Church of the Apostles in Seattle, Washington, which calls itself "a future church with an ancient faith" and builds programs to prove it (just listen to their podcasts).[4] Think of Fresh Expressions, a highly successful movement sponsored jointly by the Church of England and the Methodist Church, that is working to produce "a changing church for a changing world."[5] And think of one of its strongest supporters, Rowan Williams, the present Archbishop of Canterbury (what could be a more staid position than that?), who posts YouTube videos calling for "new ventures, new styles of church life" and "new ways of being church" that "allow people to think outside the box."[6]

The difference between influence and irrelevance will depend on how well we manage the change that lies before us. Are our church and denominational leaders ready to take the risks and lead us in new directions? Are all the rest of us willing to step out into new territory and do our parts as well?

7. Managing Change

Change can be managed—but only when it is acknowledged, accepted, and embraced. Parents, for instance, are constantly managing change, sometimes caused by major transitions in the family's history (moves, job changes, divorces, deaths in the family), and sometimes by the radical transitions that children go through as they age. Pastors are also constantly asked to manage change, whether it comes through new leadership, church crises, demographic changes in the community, new social movements, or new social structures and values. Of course, there are church leaders who fight to hold on to the past and who thus fail to respond to what's happening in their congregations and around them. But there are also great examples of pastors who are brilliantly managing upheavals and transformations in their congregations. (The TransformingTheology.org project is assembling "best practices" from these congregations and pastors and posting them to the website.)

Is it possible for denominational leaders to manage the sorts of changes in American churches that I've been describing? These are hardworking Christian executives with deep religious commitment and a professional approach to management. Unfortunately, the people around them are often pushing pretty hard to *minimize* change, so that they can preserve past structures and practices. In some cases the pressures have led to hiring Madison Avenue advertising firms, who construct expensive campaigns to market the denomination's "brand name." Perhaps you've seen some of these new advertisements on your television. The denominational execs know that their churches are facing a period of extreme crisis. At our summit meeting in May 2009, one of the denominational leaders described the situation with remarkable clarity: "We have inherited traditions that are in some cases hundreds of years old. We are being asked to keep these traditions and practices alive. Yet we know that they are under attack and many of them are struggling for their very existence. Many of our churches and other institutions may not survive the present century." Then, on a self-critical note, she named the irony: "But each of us is determined that things not collapse 'on my watch'!"

That's it in a nutshell: change may happen, but just not "on my watch." When this attitude dominates, leaders are not really preparing for the future. I want to urge the opposite response: *change can be embraced and managed*! In fact, there's an entire branch of management theory focusing on managing change. Just look at classics such as John Hayes' *The Theory and Practice of Change Management* (Palgrave Macmillan, 2002), or *Making Sense of Change Management: A Complete Guide to the Models, Tools and Techniques of Organizational Change* by Esther Cameron and Mike Green (Kogan Page, 2004). Closer to home, consider Edwin Friedman's *A Failure of Nerve: Leadership in the Age of the Quick Fix* (Seabury, 2007), with its special focus on American religious leadership. Here is a real challenge to all who would accept the title *leader*. In promotional materials for the book, the publishers give a pithy summary of Friedman's argument: "more maturity, not more data; stamina, not technique; and personal responsibility, not empathy."

Christian leaders whom I respect, while reading drafts of this section, have complained that change—change of the magnitude the church is now facing—*cannot* be managed. I have retained the term, despite their worries, because there will always be those among us who are assigned the task of managing Christian organizations, denominations, and congregations. I want to undercut the widespread view that there are only two options: preserve the past, or quit your management position. Instead, I'm calling for a new kind of manager, one who is actually *out in front* of the change, getting others to look it in the face and to begin preparing their organizations and groups for what's coming down the pike.

Clearly this is a new breed of manager, one with a different vision of management. Spencer Burke and I were discussing this new kind of leader over lunch recently, just before shooting a new segment for TheOOZE.TV. Spencer suggested that the new leaders think of themselves not as controlling events and people but as *hosting* them. Hosts invite people together, create safe settings, enable folks to feel comfortable with each other, allow differences to be expressed—and then help them deal with whatever happens during the time together. Hosting is linked to hospitality, which is a gift of the Spirit and a deep New Testament theme (see 1 Peter 4:9; Matt. 25:35). Great hosts are not top-down managers; they are geniuses at building and maintaining networks and at creating positive links with other networks. Spencer is right: a change-manager is more like a host than like a traditional CEO or a military commander.

We cannot control the changes that are already upon us, but we *can* meet them intelligently and respond to them with grace, innovation, courage, and far-sightedness. As managers and leaders, we can invite others to engage change constructively and faithfully. But it does take a very different mindset. Instead of seeking to preserve the past at any cost, we need a commitment to adapting *what we have been* as church to *what we need to be* as church in the future. This is not about ceasing to be disciples of Jesus, or replacing the true gospel with a false gospel, or "selling out" to secular humanism, or any other such evil. It is about finding a way to speak a powerful redemptive word in a context unlike any that humans have ever faced before. It takes a sort of conversion, a transformation of one's basic mindset, to be ready to take on this new task. But it's possible! Indeed, many visionary leaders, within traditional churches and outside of them, are already beginning to make the shift.

 ## An Urgent Call to Church Leaders

Heads of communions, denominational execs, bishops, and others who have responsibility for the existing Christian denominations: we call you to a fundamental change of mindset. We call you to see yourselves not as the preservers of institutional givens, but as the managers of change. You have been given the responsibility to shepherd large parts of Christ's church through one of the biggest times of social transformation that humanity has ever undergone. Many of the paradigms that you inherited are now being left behind, and new institutional and cultural paradigms are taking hold. Managing change is not about abandoning the Christian tradition, deep discipleship to Jesus Christ, or the pursuit of theological depth and richness. It doesn't mean that you stop shepherding congregations, supporting social justice ministries, and encouraging faithful obedience in all its forms. It means continuing to do all of these things—but now in a new and more effective manner, one that's appropriate for the people of today and of tomorrow.

You know the statistics from within your own denominations. You know the loss of membership, the ever-decreasing financial contributions, the large number of congregations that are teetering on the edge of collapse. You know that the other mainline denominations face similar problems. We call you no longer to implement Band-aid solutions when what are really needed are major transformations, experimental new programs, and significant shifts of resources. Together with all others who depend upon your leadership, we call you to become visionary leaders, helping the church to prepare for a stronger future.

More concretely, we call you to six specific steps to manage and support the change that is even now on our doorstep:

First, please meet with other heads of denominations and begin to speak honestly about the common challenges. Ordinary people in your churches and in our society are saying that the mainline is finished and that only evangelical and Pentecostal-charismatic churches are going to survive and thrive (and now even *their* leaders are worried). Indeed, unless you all speak with a common voice, with renewed vision and will, that prophecy will be fulfilled—either under your watch or the watch of your successors!

Second, please ask those under you, those who head large programs and boards within your denomination, to begin meeting with their colleagues in different denominations. Begin now to establish common endeavors that will help prepare the church for the changes that are even now arriving. Fighting for the private interests or the "market share" of your own denomination is not the way to strengthen the church as a whole for the future. We must focus instead on our shared proclamation and mission. Help us to *reinterpret* the great contributions of your churches in the past, so that they will continue into the future.

Third, please utilize the sound principles of change management. There are many creative ways to lead the church at a time of changing paradigms, if one is willing. Here are just a few examples:

- Divide your resources and your clergy between the task of maintaining traditional congregations and the task of developing innovative new "outside the box" programs for the future. Some percentage of pastors still must serve the aging churches. But others must be freed for radically new forms of ministry.

- Begin the sometimes painful process of investing more resources in new "best practice" forms of ministry. This will mean helping members of failing congregations to relocate to regional congregations that continue to offer traditional liturgies, music, and practices. Easing your failing churches through the process of closing is the only way to free up pastors and funds for the new forms of being church.

- Please allow the bright, young seminary students whom we are now educating to be involved in the forms of innovative ministry that they are envisioning. Trust that God is working in them as well! Allow them to form cohorts and house churches and church plants. Allow them to hold worship services in pubs (like Ikon in Dublin, Ireland), to perform street theater, to host discussion groups in office buildings, to create sidewalk Sunday schools, and to try out the other innovative ways of being church that they are even now dreaming.

- Please collect information on "best practices" and successful new programs from across the denominations, *and from outside them*, and make this information available to other pastors. If you do not take the lead in fostering and publicizing successful innovation, the church will cease to be relevant to the new world that is unfolding around us.

Fourth, instead of emphasizing your differences and the unique merits of your particular "brand" of Christianity, help us together to rediscover a "big tent" Christianity, one that emphasizes the gospel of hope that we share and not the historical differences that have divided us. You know that many of your own denominations are now splintered by questions of sexual ethics, and in particular by the destructive debate over the ordination of gay clergy. One reason why these debates are so divisive is that we are failing to voice the powerful common beliefs that hold us together.

We, the ordinary people in churches, do not need a new Creed or manifesto. We need to hear in visionary terms how the core message of the Christian tradition can still speak powerfully to our world. More and more of us are pragmatic idealists. We are not interested in detailed doctrinal disputes, in negative campaigning on behalf of traditional theological distinctions, in intolerance and exclusivity. We want relevance. But we are also quick to recognize when content evaporates and churches serve up nothing more than the re-warmed values of the surrounding culture, accompanied by the remnants of traditional Christian practice.

Listen to us also! We really believe that Jesus' message continues to be relevant to our contemporary culture, that it has something powerful to offer to a world in crisis. We believe in a gospel that is neither conservative, in the sense of exclusivist and reactionary, nor liberal, in the sense that it forsakes all content, dispenses with God, and merely covers over pop psychology or political correctness with a thin veneer of vaguely Christian language. Lead us in finding and formulating a middle way between these extremes, since we believe that the heart of Christianity lies here!

Fifth, help us to rekindle theological imagination! Help us, as pastors and ordinary people in the pews—and as those who are having trouble reconnecting with the church at all—to tell our stories using the rich theological language of our tradition. Help bring the seminaries back into the fold, so that they again become our allies as we struggle to find theological language that speaks to people where they really live. Help organize continuing education programs for pastors to give them resources and ideas for ministry in this changing world. Help creative authors to produce innovative Sunday school and adult education materials that speak to the real burning issues of our day. Better, use the most recent technologies to reach people in radically new ways. Work with us to organize high-visibility programs and working groups and make bold public statements on topics that really have the potential to change the world.

Finally, above all, don't underestimate us! We can tell when denominational statements merely mouth traditional language without really making it relevant to the contemporary world. We can tell when church documents reflect nothing more than the dominant values of surrounding society without really integrating them with the language of the Christian hope. If you let us, we can help you decide what is relevant and what is not. We can help you to be leaders who host new encounters, who name the changes and identify the challenges they bring. We will work with you and support you. In return, as leaders it's your responsibility to continually step out in front of the rest of us, into those risky places where no one knows for sure what the right answers are. Rise up and really be our leaders!

Part Two

Theologies That Can Transform the Church

8. Don't Give Up on the Church!

As we've seen, mainline churches today are facing a crisis greater than at any time since the founding of Christianity in the United States. These churches, once the staple of American religious life, have undergone a steady decline in membership for over four decades, and the situation has now reached a critical point for many mainline denominations. Large numbers of congregations are fighting to survive. Some experts predict that *over half* of the mainline congregations that exist today will be forced to close their doors over the coming two decades. (The situation in evangelical, Pentecostal, and charismatic churches is not so dire, but it does show some of the same tendencies.)

Let's recap what in the American situation has changed so radically that once prosperous churches and denominations are now struggling mightily. Of the many contributing factors, a few in particular strike me as especially important. (The first two points were suggested by my friend and frequent co-author Steven Knapp, and I quote his words verbatim):

1. "People no longer believe that church attendance is socially necessary, that is, necessary for the social health and perhaps even the economic survival of individuals and their family, either because churches provide the only context for social interaction or because they are necessary to the relationships on which careers and businesses depend."

2. "People no longer believe that church attendance provides the only or the most important means of establishing and maintaining a sufficiently strong connection with God, however such a connection is specifically understood (for example, in terms of salvation, spiritual health, a life of meaning, etc.)."

3. Many of the institutions that once stood at the center of our society are equally endangered, such as the Boy Scouts and Girl Scouts, Kiwanis, and Masonic groups. On the whole, Americans just don't join institutions

we used to. Instead, we hang out with family and friends, use electronic entertainment, shop, or go online. For how many people today is church coffee hour the social highlight of their week? Many people prefer to watch reality TV in order to see humans "as they really are."

4. The classic modes of church teaching—reciting together and listening to a preacher talk for twenty minutes—are no longer effective modes for communicating important information for many Americans. (Even classroom teachers today show videos and use PowerPoint.) For many, hymn-singing no longer has the force it once did.

5. The traditional church was a family unit. It not only included mom and dad and the three kids, but also grandparents, aunts and uncles, and other extended family members. By contrast, today there are fissures even in the nuclear family. No longer centered on multi-generational family units, mainline churches struggle to retain their members.

6. Most of us do not live in one place long enough to put down real roots. When three generations of your family were hatched, matched, and dispatched in the local church, it was a pretty strong magnet to keep you involved. Now families may move seven times or more before the kids leave for college.

7. Our communities are not only in continual flux; they are massively more diverse in beliefs, values, and social identities. Church communities in the U.S. used to be highly homogenous; difference was dealt with by having lots of congregations. Fewer churches means a greater diversity in socio-economic status, ethnicity, education, ethical convictions, and political beliefs in the remaining congregations. Diversity often makes people uncomfortable, so it is no surprise that many are voting with their feet.

8. Pastors today are generally not viewed as moral authorities in their communities, and theologians do not speak for and to the nation. Paul Tillich's *Courage to Be* was a bestseller, and Reinhold Niebuhr was on the cover of *Newsweek*. Walter Rauschenbusch's *Christianity and the Social Crisis* was a national bestseller for three years beginning in 1907. Dr. Martin Luther King Jr. spoke not only as a civil rights leader but also as a pastor. With a few notable exceptions, church leaders and theologians no longer play that prophetic role in today's world.

9. We are no longer blending powerful theologies with transformative ministries in the world. Churches and denominations that are actively involved in "social justice ministries" are often unable to give a theological

rationale for their actions that people find moving and compelling. By contrast, the theologies that really move people today tend to be more private and personal. They focus more on individual salvation and individual religious experience; they tend to separate the church from the world; and many of the popular ones defend the superiority of Christian belief by denigrating its competitors.

In short, the social beliefs and networks that once motivated church attendance and involvement are now under attack, and many institutions are crumbling. Effective answers to the current situation will require us either to breathe new life into existing institutions or to invent radically new forms of Christian community.

Perhaps you are optimistic that we will be able to respond to the challenges facing the church, or perhaps you despair, wondering if it's even worth trying. Perhaps you've become cynical about institutional religion as a whole. But as you begin to develop your own solutions, I would urge you not to give up on the church altogether. Here are three reasons:

First, we frequently hear people say, "I am spiritual but not religious." What's interesting is that, both in our own day and throughout history, when people are really seriously spiritual, they seek out communities of like-minded people to deepen their spiritual practices, to support each other in their practice, and to try to understand the insights that result. Buddhists are often cited as radical spiritual individualists and held up as models of private spirituality, but it's not true. Spiritual teachers, sanghas, Dharma talks, and the guidance of a community have always played important roles in Buddhist practice. It is very, very rare to find deep spiritual practice that lacks communal support. Even the monks and nuns whose deep personal spirituality so many of us admire depend on a precisely defined system of social support and encouragement. People whose spirituality lacks any communal support usually drift from one spiritual tradition to another or eventually abandon their spiritual practice altogether.

Second, the idea of a purely individualistic Christian practice—Christianity without church—divides the "visible" church from the "invisible" church. One might be tempted to dismiss the entire visible church as worthless, claiming that one's own practice or theology alone represents the true or "invisible" church. But how can that be? The church is the incarnation of the Spirit of Christ in any given age, the body of Christ when Jesus no longer walks the earth. For better or worse, in its various communal manifestations it becomes his representative on earth: "For where two or three are gathered in my name, I am there among them" (Matt. 18:20). We can never fully separate the "true" church from the visible church. So, although we may need to innovate existing structures, sometimes in radical ways, in the long run the fate of the visible church as a whole continues to matter; we can never "just leave it behind." In the next few pages I hope to show that rekindling theology is one way to help re-establish these connections.

> *If we try, we may succeed. But if we do not try at all, it is certain that we will fail.*

There's one last reason not to give up on the church: if we try, we may succeed. But if we do not try at all, it is *certain* that we will fail. In this book I condone many of the experiments that currently are taking place independent of denominations, as people try to live out new ways of hearing and responding to Jesus' call outside traditional church structures (and sometimes *far* aside). If our innovations are to keep stride with the rapid pace of cultural change, these and even bolder experiments will be necessary. Still, if you think about it, whatever new forms of thought and practice "two or three" of Jesus' followers engage in are hypotheses about what the future of the church might look like. Their successes are successes for *all of us* who are on the Way.

9. Transformative Theologies

aced with the challenges outlined in the previous chapter, one is inclined to a rather dark view of future prospects for mainline churches. Here's what the dark view looks like: the church trains its best and brightest candidates for ministry in seminaries, giving them three years of academic course work and, usually, some sort of internship experience. Then they are to go out to serve and grow the church, doing everything possible to keep their little congregations alive. Since most of their church attendees are over the age of sixty-five, the young clergy person is really being asked to build a ministry that is largely geared to the needs of this population, while somehow managing to attract new youth, young adults, and families at the same time. No wonder there is clergy burnout!

We're sending our best and our brightest out into the world with the mandate of conserving existing structures. But what they dream of when they enter seminary and begin taking my classes—and hopefully are still dreaming when they're finished with these classes!—is to find new ways of being "church" in today's world. These are fantastic, visionary men and women who want to renew the church and help transform society. What does the church do? It places them under immense pressure to maintain the existing structures. With this assignment, how are they to reach those who are leaving the church in droves? How are they to reach the seekers and those who are drifting further and further away from traditional institutional forms of religion? As one younger minister told me recently, "It's as if we're being sent out to provide hospice care to ailing congregations. Don't they realize that most of these 'patients' just aren't going to recover?"

New books flooding the market talk about ways for the church to become (or stay) relevant to today's world. Many, including those listed under "For Further Reading" on page 181, offer valuable concrete suggestions and I commend you to read and learn from them. Well-known speakers crisscross America lecturing on the same topic. These books and speakers describe the dramatic cultural changes that have created a new environment for the church today.

Tripp Fuller interprets these cultural changes as "missiological barriers"—contextual challenges to communicating the gospel. Some individuals and denominations are employing creative methods in order to get their message through despite these challenges. Together with many others, however, we are worried that innovative techniques by themselves don't go far enough unless they also free the gospel from its imprisonment within modern ways of thinking. Is it enough to add contemporary music or a few technological enhancements when the message is still couched in terms of absolute foundations and sets of mutually exclusive categories? Sure, let's experiment boldly with new forms of worship and community, new ways of being church. But we must *also* do the hard work of freeing the Good News from modern, Western (and sometimes even distinctively American) assumptions with which it has become confused. A lot more is at stake than designing a few new programs. It's about what and how we believe, which, as you now know, means it's about *theologies*.

> *A transformative theology is a powerful statement of what you believe, one that guides and motivates transformative action in the world.*

This challenge is going to take some serious thinking. It will take the involvement of all of us, from the most famous heads of denominations to the humblest church attendees, if Christians are to succeed at formulating *transformative theologies* for this new age. A transformative theology is *a powerful statement of what you believe, one that can guide and motivate transformative action in the world.* After all, no number of church-growth strategies—Sunday school curricula, contemporary music, innovative social and community-building activities for adults, sexy new modes of youth ministry, crafty uses of mass media—will be sufficient if we cannot tell a convincing story of what it means to be Christian in today's world.

A disembodied, head-only theology is an empty husk, an invitation to hypocrisy and pride. Genuine theologies are always embodied. They are what you believe with a passion and what you most deeply want your life to manifest. Genuine theologies lead to worship, and worship leads to action. I often tell audiences, "Whatever you get red in the face and passionate about when you talk, that's your real theology. That's where your heart is. The other stuff may be someone else's theology, but it isn't yours." Be careful when you apply this criterion, though—it's likely to take you to some pretty honest places, and you may be surprised by the results.

Consider a contrast. It may be that a business needs no more rationale for existing than the observation, "Well, we can make money this way." But Christians must "be ready to make your defense to anyone who demands from you an accounting for the hope that is in you" (1 Peter 3:15). We need to interpret this verse not as a call to use argumentative techniques designed to compel others to "come on over to our side." Instead, its primary call is *to give a self-accounting*—that is, to be able to explain our own strongest motivations and reasons. To do this, we have to make sense of our own actions and convictions *to ourselves* first. Only then will we have any chance of making sense to other people, such as our friends and colleagues.

 ## Two Warring Camps

Sadly, the American church today tends to divide into two camps when it comes to theology, with each viewing the other as a dangerous opponent. One camp wants to use more traditional language and to define itself in more traditional terms. For example, there are some in conservative evangelical churches—but not only there—who argue that continuing to use the traditional language is the indispensable mark of a Christian. And yet it's becoming harder and harder to *translate* this language so that it speaks in sophisticated ways to the real problems and needs of today's world. How do I help my children deal with the complex moral and ethical choices with which their social world confronts them? When is an economic system consistent with basic Christian principles and when is it unjust? What does the gospel have to say about using stem cell technologies in medical research? How should I view the other religions of the world? Until I can make the necessary translations, I'm not really applying the traditional language, however frequently I may cite it.

The other camp is able to make strong values statements about the contemporary world—about race, gender, and class issues, or about justice, peace, and equality. It specializes in being relevant. But members of this camp have a harder time connecting their admittedly urgent, and often moving concerns and causes to the received language of Christianity, to its founding texts and its traditions. We as listeners, but also they as speakers, need to be able to answer the question: how did they get from *there* to *here*?[1] Like many others, I care deeply about equal rights and freedom of speech, and I want to work for reasonable democracy over fanaticism. I oppose oppression and injustice. But what does it mean to care about these things *as a Christian*? Is there anything uniquely Christian about these values, or are they fully universal? We know that Muslims and Hindus also give arguments against oppression and injustice. How do we link our activism with core Christian ideas such as creation, salvation, and beliefs about Christ?

This "two camps" mentality is making it difficult for folks to formulate their own transformative theologies. As long as the two camps represent an either/or choice, the church will not be able to speak with a unified and powerful voice to the contemporary world situation. We will continue to be rent asunder—the one side condemning the "secular humanism" and immoralities of our day and calling us back to first-century beliefs and practices, the other side becoming more and more politically engaged but less and less able to ground the activism in the language of our tradition.

Returning to "Big Tent" Christianity

There are increasing signs that the rigid opposition between these two sides is beginning to abate. Younger Christians across the spectrum of churches are no longer willing to be pigeonholed into one of the two camps. The old battle lines no longer seem compelling. "Why can't I be evangelical and also hold progressive political convictions?" a student asks me. "Why should liberals be the only ones who get to talk about social justice issues?" At the same time, mainline Christians are finding powerful grounds in the gospels and the Christian tradition for their ongoing concern with issues of race, gender, class, and social oppression.

These are signs of an exciting return to a "big tent" Christianity. No one is urging that we create one mega-denomination or write a creed that all are expected to sign. But it's getting easier to recognize once again our common features as followers of Jesus Christ. While we may follow the one we call Teacher and Lord in different ways, with different language and emphases, depending on our age, location, and social world, we're all under a single tent. Together we constitute the same body of Christ.

"Big tent" Christianity brings to my mind the picture of the old revival meetings, sometimes called "tent meetings" or "camp meetings," that used to take place across the United States. When a famous preacher came to town, a huge tent would be set up in a nearby field and folks from all the different churches would come together to pray, sing, and worship. They'd hear the call to repentance and deeper discipleship, and many would re-commit themselves to their faith. These meetings were a huge part of the growth of Christianity in America; they helped to produce what's known as the Second Great Awakening (1790–1840s). They still continue in some places in the country, though most revival meetings are now held in church buildings.

I associate renewal and passionate personal commitment with "big tent" Christianity. Coming together under one tent also suggests setting our differences aside in order to emphasize what we share in common. Commentators have described Barack Obama's approach to his campaign and to the presidency as a "big tent" approach to politics. He's clearly trying to build broader coalitions, to get folks to work together for real change—even when they differ sharply over other matters. The "big tent" Christianity that I've been describing will only work if we achieve something like the attitude to which President Obama has been calling the nation. Otherwise we'll never be willing to stand together, even for a few hours, in order to be counted as the one church of Jesus Christ.

 ## Don't Just Talk about It: Do It!

There is danger in spending all one's time describing the space in which theology *might* be done, but never getting around to actually doing any theology. Sadly, many people who are called theologians succumb to this temptation. Metaphorically speaking, they are like builders who talk about why houses should be built but who never actually get around to building any. Such theologians draw up detailed (book-length!) architectural plans to say how a theological house might be built. They locate the house that should be built amongst all the other neighborhoods of our day: the disciplines, the social needs and institutions, the media, the various religions, the problems of relativism and reductionism, the changing nature of human existence, and the like. They even describe the details of what a "systematic Christian theology for our day" would look like—if anyone ever wrote it. But, in the end, it seems that for many religious scholars, including (sadly) many who are known as theologians, theology is the house that the *other* guy is supposed to build.

Academic theologians call this discourse about "The House That Nobody Built" *theological methodology*. In graduate school and for years afterwards, I was a great expert on theological methodology—chief among sinners, if you want me to boast. I spent years working on my dissertation and first book, *Explanation from Physics to Theology: An Essay in Rationality and Religion*. I learned all the ways that one can use natural science and social science and the humanities and philosophy and history in order to dictate what theology must be and do (were anyone ever to get around to doing any). And yet, if you dig that book out of a dusty library somewhere, you'll find that it contains precious little theology.

 ## Learning from Experience

I well remember the day I finally understood this lesson. I had just successfully defended the doctoral dissertation before a group of philosophy and religious studies professors at Yale University. Afterward, as we walked out across the old quad at Yale, R.I.G. Hughes, a famous philosopher of quantum physics and not himself a religious believer, said to me, "Well, all this talk *about* theology is very nice and all. But what do you actually believe about God? Who is God?" At the time, it was a rather deflating comment for a newly minted Ph.D. to hear. But later, as I reflected on the implicit criticism, I realized how right he was. I hadn't really said anything much at all about who God was, despite all the talk about *how* to answer the question. As a specialist in what theology should be, did I even know what I believed about God?

The same issue arises all over again when it comes to what you believe about Jesus. Again, I learned the lesson the hard way. In those days Hans Frei was one of the best-known theologians at Yale. One day when I entered the department he was standing on the stairs. He beckoned me with his forefinger, which was always the sign that he wanted one of his advisees to come up to his office for a talking-to. I nervously followed him up the stairs. After a few polite inquiries into my recent work on theological methodology, he began to explain the dangers of that quest. He walked me back through the decades of disputes about what theology should be (if anyone ever got around to doing it), summarizing the famous books by Langdon Gilkey (*Naming the Whirlwind* and *Reaping the Whirlwind*) and David Tracy (*Blessed Rage for Order* and *The Analogical Imagination*). Gradually he began to convince me that none of these authors were actually producing any profound and enduring theologies of their own. And then he said to me—I remember the words verbatim—"You are not a theologian until you have written a Christology."

The words hit home, and I have never forgotten them. The christological question—What was the nature and work of Jesus Christ?—is *the* central question that every Christian has to answer. I now build it into the heart of my work with future ministers. When students write their Credos, their belief statements, I ask them to answer the question that Jesus posed to his disciples in Matthew 16:15: "But who do *you* say that I am?" (You will not find the italics in your Bible, but you *should* hear them in the question).

You have not built a theological house, walked into it, and started to live there until you have attempted to give some answer to that question. It's not enough to be able to discourse on the history of doctrines of Christ or to list Scriptures about Christ or to compile quotations from other authors on the topic. We need to answer the question, pure and simple, the way that Jesus posed it: "But who do *you* say that I am?" The answer doesn't need footnotes. It doesn't have to be in Hebrew, Greek, Latin, and German. Your answer today may be different from the answer you give next week or next year—in fact, it probably *should* be different, since you will have more and different life experiences at a later time. But, if you choose to use the name "Christian" to describe yourself, this is the question that stands before you at every waking minute. And in fact, every thought and action in a person's life implicitly helps to identify what answer he or she is giving to that question.

Now this is not a book that is going to tell you what is the right answer to the christological question, the question about Jesus. You'll find dozens of books that do that. Instead, *I'm asking you to spend some serious time with the question in all its complexity*, so that you can learn to answer it more deeply and powerfully.

"But why?" someone responds. "The answer is simple: 'Jesus is Lord and Savior.' That's all you need to know." Are you sure? The more significant you think Jesus is, the harder you should be thinking about what your claims mean and imply. Perhaps if your answer is "just a good guy," you can be forgiven for not giving the question another thought; why should you? But if you believe there is something special, even unique, about Jesus, you need to be reading and talking with others to get clear on your beliefs and reasons.

Let me say this more strongly: the church is great at giving answers, but not so good at understanding the questions. We need to provide space for folks, not just for "seekers" *but also for believers*, to wrestle with what they believe and why. Then each of us needs to have the courage to work out what we really think—even if it's not the politically correct answer in our particular context. Remember: you can't satisfy everyone. There will *always* be people on one side of you who think your doctrine of Christ is "too low" (doesn't emphasize Jesus' divinity enough), and people on the other side who think it's "too high" (doesn't emphasize the humanity of Jesus enough). At the end of the day, don't you just have to work out the best answer you can give, whether others like it or not, and tell people honestly what you think?

10. Learning to Find Your Theological Voice

T here's a widespread misconception that you have to leave your everyday world and go away somewhere in order to work out your answers to questions about religion and faith. In fact, the most common misconception is that you have to go away to seminary. Seminaries are places where people like me issue driver's licenses or something that allow you to do theology. Then there's a second misconception: the belief that theologians come in only two flavors—pastors and academic theologians, a.k.a. seminary professors. Only people with special credentials can produce theology. On this view, theology is what pastors and professors create—books and sermons, presumably, and nothing else.

It should be obvious that I am challenging these stereotypes from the ground up. They are *so* wrong that there is no point in trying to patch them up here and there. The whole paradigm needs to shift; we need to start all over again. In fact, if it were possible I would get rid of the word *theology* altogether and substitute another for it. The trouble is, there is no other word that will suffice. When you can't do without a word, you have to fight to redeem it. *Theology* is in the same category as *Christian, disciple,* and *church.* We need all these words or else we'll get locked into a conspiracy of silence about things that we just have to talk about.

Make Your Beliefs Conscious

So here's the starting point: *everything* that a Christian does already expresses a theology, explicitly or implicitly. Instead of being neatly locked up in seminaries and pastors' studies, theology is ubiquitous. You simply can't avoid doing it unless you abandon belief in God altogether. As you can see, this starting point stands as far from the stereotype about theology as one could possibly get. I also think it's true.

Here's an analogy. Remember the old debate about how much of one's life is relevant to one's discipleship or Christian faith? People seem to believe that God *really cares* about where they are during that one hour on Sunday mornings, whereas there are other hours during the week when God isn't paying attention in quite the same way. Pastors and teachers are always trying to overcome people's natural tendency to divide their lives up into the "sacred" or religious parts on the one hand, and the "secular" parts on the other. For followers of Jesus, *everything* one does is relevant to Christian discipleship. This makes discipleship pretty earthy; it de-spiritualizes it in a way that's healthy and productive and appropriate to the New Testament.

But whatever is true of discipleship is true of theology as well. Discipleship is like driving the car, and theology is the manual that describes how the engine works. Theology manuals have to speak to every aspect of lived Christian life. That makes theology pretty earthy too. Some people love to spiritualize it—right out of their lives. Genuine theologies are embodied; they have implications for life. And everything we do hints at what our real theology is.

> *The goal is to make implicit beliefs about God conscious, explicit, and intentional.*

If all that we do hints at our real beliefs, then clearly most of what we believe will tend to be implicit rather than fully conscious. *The goal is to lift our implicit beliefs about God above the threshold of consciousness, so that they become explicit and intentional.* Only then can we examine our beliefs to see which ones actually stand up to scrutiny. Believers need to engage in this process together for the same reasons we have conversations with other people. Of course, we can always *guess* what other people are thinking and what's motivating their actions. But unless we ask them, our guesses are often wrong. Likewise, sometimes we figure out our own reasons only when we're asked about them. "Why did you do *that*?" my wife asks, and I realize that I have no idea at all why I did what I did! Assumptions only come to the surface when people talk together about their actions and beliefs.

The same is true for religious beliefs. By their very nature they are woven into the deepest fabric of our being; they represent our most deeply held views and values about existence. We bring them to the surface in order to check them, alter the unhealthy ones, and reconsider those that have become implausible.

Examples to Get You Started

As someone who does this for a living I have to say that, at the unconscious level, people hold some pretty amazing beliefs about God. For years it's been my job and passion to talk with a very wide range of people about their unspoken religious assumptions and to help turn them into explicit theologies. This work is more like therapy or pastoral counseling than you might expect. Take just one common example: An amazing number of people believe (without having ever examined their assumptions very carefully) that God is primarily in the business of being dissatisfied with them. They also believe that, if they are very good and try very hard, they can at least *decrease* God's continuing displeasure with them a little bit. Since the Reformation, people have called this attitude "works righteousness," and many great arguments have been composed against it. But until people bring their underlying assumptions about this vindictive God to consciousness, until they compare the punishing God with the "Abba, Father" whom Jesus proclaimed (Mark 14:36; cf. Rom. 8:15; Gal. 4:6), they find it difficult to evaluate and correct them. (Perhaps we are afraid to look too closely at our hidden beliefs about God because we don't really want to own them as ours.)

As soon as we make our theological assumptions conscious, we can compare them with other ways of thinking about God and decide which are really the more adequate. Consider another example: the (sadly, widespread) view that God is primarily an angry, even wrathful God. Some people were brought up to believe in a vindictive God, perhaps through Sunday school or parochial school or sermons they heard. Others may have internalized the anger and judgment of a parent and projected it onto the heavens as the dangerous wrath of an angry God. Still others may have assumed from all the talk about their need for salvation and how they would end up in hell if they didn't do certain things that God must always be angry. It's amazing to see what can happen when these same people (who are often church members) reflect on what it means that God views us through the lens of grace rather than only through the lens of our failures and imperfections. It's one thing to affirm the *theory* that God's fundamental nature is love, quite another thing to internalize it.

Our religious lives are packed with unspoken (and often unconscious) assumptions that don't stand up to the light of day. As long as they are kept hidden, they will massively influence our religious practice. Other examples I frequently encounter include:

- the belief that if I'm good enough I'll go to heaven (also known as "salvation by works");
- the belief that pastors and religious leaders have it all figured out and never have doubts; which leads to:
- the belief that if I just let them tell me what to believe, I'll be fine;
- the belief that all the religions really say the same thing, so that the specific beliefs of (say) Christianity really don't matter that much;
- the belief that Jesus' fundamental message was that we should all just be nice to each other;
- the belief that churches are places where "the good people" meet;
- the belief that all that really matters is that we save souls;
- the belief that all that really matters is that we take care of the poor and needy.

Finding more adequate ways to view God and God's attitude toward humanity is the necessary first step toward changing that relationship. I can't emphasize enough how powerful and liberating this transformation is—it's the stuff of redemption.

Of course, beliefs by themselves are not sufficient; *I am not reducing being a disciple to getting your beliefs straight.* Nor are all our beliefs under our conscious control. Frequently people find that they subconsciously ascribe certain features to God (or Christ or church) that they do not want to consciously affirm, and yet they may be unable to change them. A girl who has been abused by her father may be convinced in her mind that God is not like a human father, but she may be unable really to believe this until she has experienced a safe, loving, accepting, grace-filled relationship with a human male. I may *will* to accept God's grace, so that I no longer have to win God's favor through my own works, but I may continually fail to live in this grace until I have known a human relationship that is permeated by grace and unconditional love. Thinking about what we believe, reflecting on what does and doesn't really make sense, is a crucial part of the Christian life—which is why the pervasive absence of this kind of reflection in churches today is such an enormous problem. But reflection alone is not sufficient. So, for the record: although this book is about learning to think about what you believe, I am not claiming that theology is *all* that the Christian life is about.

The Seven Core Christian Questions

So where do you start when you want to find your own theological voice? People who have done youth ministry, as I have, know that you don't dump the entire complexity of Christian discipleship onto an elementary or middle school student. For young Christians, discipleship starts with just a few central ideas that they can concentrate on and practice. Adults, by contrast, can take on some pretty complex things. But even we have to learn them in stages, a step at a time. Think of Paul's distinction between milk and solid food (1 Cor. 3:2), repeated by the author of Hebrews (5:12-14).

In theology as in the rest of life, there's a natural progression. We start with beliefs that are very basic and stable for ourselves. These are the core convictions, the ones we have built our lives around—we could even say the ones for which we'd be prepared to die. Time and time again I've found people who weren't sure they *had* any real religious beliefs gradually discover that they in fact hold some really deep Christian convictions. Then, after we've learned to express and formulate our beliefs in the clear areas, it's relatively easy to extend them outwards into fields we may not have thought much about before. Later, as we get better at integrating Scripture and tradition with the contemporary world situation and its challenges, we can move into increasingly difficult and complex areas.

Here is my proposal for beginning to think theologically. Over the centuries, great Christian leaders have identified a number of central topics within the Christian tradition. Let's call them the Seven Core Christian Questions. They are easy to list:

- Who is God?
- Who is Jesus, called the Christ
- Who is the Spirit, or the Holy Spirit?
- What is humanity? What does it mean to be human?
- What is the problem of sin, and what does salvation mean?

- What is the nature and function of the church?
- What is the future in which we hope and for which we long?

Each of these Seven Core Christian Questions has a big name, an -*ology*, by which it is traditionally identified. They are:

- *Theology* or "theology proper": questions about who God is and how God is related to the world.
- *Christology*: questions about the person and the teaching of Jesus and about how he is related to God.
- *Pneumatology*: questions about who the Spirit is, the Spirit's role in creation and the church, and (in traditional language) the relationship of Spirit to Father and Son.
- *Anthropology*: questions about what it means to be human: how are we like other animals? How are we different? What is the "image of God" (*imago Dei*) in us?
- *Soteriology*: questions about what salvation is. What is the problem of sin that it addresses? What is the human role and what is God's role? What has God done to overcome the problem of sin, and what is Jesus' role in this solution? What kind of discipleship does salvation produce? How is salvation related to sanctification, that is, growing more God-like or Christ-like over time?
- *Ecclesiology*: questions about the church. What is its mission? What are its defining characteristics? How is it like and unlike other human associations?
- *Eschatology*: questions about "last things." What happens after we die? What is the final fate of the universe? What are heaven, "the second coming," and eternal life with God?

So now we have a new definition of theology: *theology consists of all attempts to answer these core Christian questions for ourselves in light of the contemporary world*—contemporary experience, contemporary social and political realities, contemporary science, and other philosophies and religions. When churches begin to empower folks to wrestle with these questions, the results will be revolutionary—in personal discipleship, in congregational life, and in the church's ministry in the world. That's why the Transforming Theology project has as its basic motto, "Rekindling theological imagination: developing transformative theologies for church and society."

Building Church Programs from Theology Outward

Now let's switch from the individual dimension to the level of the corporate Christian life. Whatever you might think, churches are actually quite good at building programs. Youth ministry is a great example. Good youth ministry programs today often have more bells and whistles than your iPhone does. Senior pastors, taking their cue from the field of youth ministry (as many pastors have learned to do), then build equally impressive-looking programs for adults. The result can be a brilliant array of fine programs. This is a good thing.

Unfortunately, we're not as good when it comes to giving theological reasons for *why* we offer the programs that we do. We expect individuals to "be ready to make your defense [reason, *apologia*] . . . for the hope that is in you" (1 Peter 3:15). Shouldn't we expect churches (and denominations, for that matter) to be able to do the same? Yet as the Transforming Theology project has surveyed dozens and dozens of church websites, we have found that lots of churches seem to be having a really hard time with this task. Not all, of course. I am not a member of Rick Warren's Saddleback Church near Los Angeles. But I am impressed when even their Google listing gives a link called "What We Believe" that I can click on.[1] Can you imagine how powerful it would be if every mainline church had a link on its homepage called, "What We Believe," explaining how all of their ministries, whether in the church and in the community, grow out of their core Christian convictions and the history of the church's reading of Scripture?

The next urgent step in developing transformative theologies, then, is learning how to give theological reasons or justifications for why we do the things we do together as church. Doing this is equally urgent *wherever* your church lies on the spectrum from conservative to liberal. Bruce Sanguin does a beautiful job of explaining this concept in his interview on HomebrewedChristianity.com.[2] Bruce pastors Canadian Memorial Church, a progressive church with a concern for social justice ministries. He sees no reason why progressive churches shouldn't have their own core identity, their own list of "non-negotiables." His include the centrality of Jesus Christ and the gospel, but also the open table for communion and an activist understanding of the "proclamation of peace." Bruce calls every congregation to identify its non-negotiables, which provide its stability and self-definition.

Powerful ministries grow from this place. When nothing is non-negotiable for a church, one fears that nothing is believed with depth and conviction either.

Imagine Martin Luther in the Twenty-First Century

Consider the example of a young Catholic monk in the early sixteenth century. Martin Luther saw that church practice had drifted far from the teachings and model of the church's Founder. Money seemed to rule major church decisions, and too often ecclesial power was equated with political power. Particularly abhorrent to him was the selling of indulgences. Church doctrine at the time taught that a person must spend some time in purgatory after death to be "purged" of sins and purified for entrance into heaven. For the price of a major donation to the church, priests and bishops were willing to promise that they would shorten the time in purgatory for family members—but only if the price was right.

In contrast to the pattern in many congregations today, Luther knew that reform had to start with a powerful theological platform, with statements of shared belief. He went public by nailing a list of ninety-five theses to the door of the church in Wittenberg, Germany. He offered no sociological analysis, consulted no focus groups, and prepared no action plan. Instead, Luther listed and defended his central theological commitments, offering what was in essence an outline of his overall interpretation of Christian discipleship. Hear just a few examples:

- "When our Lord and Master Jesus Christ said, 'Repent' (Matt. 4:17), he willed the entire life of believers to be one of repentance. . . . The penalty of sin remains as long as the hatred of self (that is, true inner repentance), namely till our entrance into the kingdom of heaven."

- "Furthermore, it does not seem proved, either by reason or by Scripture, that souls in purgatory are outside the state of merit, that is, unable to grow in love. . . . Nor does it seem proved that souls in purgatory, at least not all of them, are certain and assured of their own salvation, even if we ourselves may be entirely certain of it. . . . A Christian who is truly contrite seeks and loves to pay penalties for his sins; the bounty of indulgences, however,

relaxes penalties and causes men to hate them—at least it fur-
nishes occasion for hating them."

- "Away, then, with all those prophets who say to the people of
Christ, 'Peace, peace,' and there is no peace! (Jer. 6:14). Blessed
be all those prophets who say to the people of Christ, 'Cross,
cross,' and there is no cross! Christians should be exhorted to be
diligent in following Christ, their Head, through penalties, death
and hell. And thus be confident of entering into heaven through
many tribulations rather than through the false security of peace
(Acts 14:22)."[3]

The pattern today is for a church to post a brief mission statement summarizing its theological commitments and motivations on its website (and
that's indeed a good start). Denominations, mission boards, and other Christian organizations tend to do the same. They then turn to the "real business"
of running the organization. But consider again the contrast with Luther. He
continued to develop and deepen his theology and to publish it in every genre
that he could find or invent. He wrote a series of disputations; a longer and
shorter catechism (so that others could learn and internalize these beliefs);
commentaries on a vast number of books of the Bible; and more sermons
than most of us could ever imagine reading. He even came up with a short,
snappy phrase, short enough to post on a billboard, that summarized the
central message of his entire theology: *justification by grace through faith*.

Clearly Luther wanted to be an agent of change in the church and in
society. But he knew that just altering one or another part of current Christian practice would be superficial and temporary. The reforms had to stem
from fundamental changes in the church's understanding of its Founder—
Christ—and his core teaching.

Luther was right! It's not that one shouldn't design programs and seek
to be effective; that too is part of the job description for Christian leaders. Youth ministers have to construct programs that are attractive to the
kids in the church and the community or they won't come. Congregations
need social activities that invite people in; they need a rich array of activities that help to keep the community vibrant; and as corporations, whether
large or small, they also need smart business management. The management
demands for regional church bodies, annual conferences, international mission boards, and huge denominations grow exponentially more complex. *But*

all these activities are worthless if we cannot give a clear corporate state-ment of what we believe and live for. Good actions and good management techniques alone are not sufficient.

I have been writing this book with a great team of young researchers. For weeks we have been scouring Christian books, magazines, publicity bro-chures, and websites. We've been looking for statements of the theological understandings that undergird prominent ministries, churches, denomina-tional programs, and Christian social ministries. All these groups are clear on their Christian heritage; all cite Scripture, at least minimally, to defend their existence and to explain their motivation. But in a surprising number of cases, that's as far as it goes. Often their materials say that faith is the foundation of what they do and that their ministries are meant to be mani-festations of the love of God. People know that complex programs without love are empty, "a noisy gong or a clanging cymbal" (1 Cor. 13:1). They know that Jesus is somehow the model (though many mainline churches are surprisingly shy to say this outright). Still, my colleagues and I are finding a huge gap between the (often pretty minimal) theological principles and the detailed action plans, programs, and curricula of churches and other Christian ministries.

What has gone wrong? Why this resounding silence? Perhaps progres-sive Christians and people in mainline churches fear that if they list core beliefs and theological assumptions, people will think they are fundamental-ists. Perhaps they fear that others will view them as exclusivist or dogmatic. Obviously, people are tempted to stick to the level of simple principles ("God is love" or "injustice is wrong"), which no one can dispute. They then want to jump straight from a simple faith (however sincere it may be) to complicated ministries and program construction. But what's to bridge the gap? On what principles and assumptions do we construct our intricate pro-grams and ministries? Many churches and para-church organizations appear to have no idea how to go about constructing the bridges from their core Christian convictions to the ministries in which they're investing their time, energy, and resources.

We need a simple yet powerful place to start.

11. Theology as Telling the Story

Modern assumptions are clearly part of what's getting in the way of developing vibrant theologies for our day. Remember: in the modern paradigm, one's beliefs must fit together into a system of propositions—a system that builds up from indubitable foundations through logical inferences to conclusions that should be compelling for all rational agents. "Modern" theological systems are like the skyscrapers in New York City: their girders are driven deep down into immovable bedrock; their structures are constructed according to scientific principles of engineering that ensure structural integrity; and they rise, story upon story, to objectively measurable heights.

As we saw, postmodern talk about belief works very differently. It's much more simple, and personally more demanding: we begin by trying to tell our story. As theologians like Hans Frei and James McClendon have emphasized, we recite a narrative—in this case, a narrative of how God's call and action have intersected with our own lives. Brian McLaren puts it beautifully:

> Rather than trying to capture timeless truth in objective statements systematized in analytical outlines and recorded in books and institutionalized in schools and denominations, narrative theology embraces, preserves, and reflects on the stories of people and communities involved in the romance of God.[1]

I want God to be at the center of my life, and I believe that God's will and nature are powerfully visible through Jesus Christ. Language about God will therefore pop up frequently as I recite (to myself and others) the ever-evolving story of my life. Once the problematic modern assumptions are off the table, why should I be afraid of this fact? Is it somehow embarrassing that I can't tell my life history without using the words *God*, *grace*, *resurrection, redemption,* and *eschatological hope*? I would rather confront the hidden standards of political correctness that are causing the embarrassment than give up speaking about God. Some such "PC" standards must be at work, right? Why else would so many of my fellow mainline Christians have become so silent about their beliefs? (One of my first church memories is the gusto with which the adults in my Presbyterian church used to sing the refrain, "I love to tell the story, 'twill be my theme in glory, to tell the old, old story of Jesus and his love.")

Some readers have interpreted the terms *story* and *narrative* to mean "fiction." When I ask you to start doing theology by learning to tell your own story with and before God, *I am not asking you to believe that it is false!* Doing theology means consciously reflecting about your real life as it has become intertwined with a real God. The trouble is that people are really good at repeating statements about God—usually statements they've learned in church—but they're not as good at linking these statements richly and deeply to their own lives. So just to be clear: the emphasis on storytelling in this chapter is not meant to encourage you to talk *as if* there were a God (while all the time really knowing that there isn't). Instead, it's the first step toward making statements about God that you really believe and that really do something in the world.

 ## Telling Theological Stories at the Personal Level

Telling our personal stories should be the easiest of all, so I start here. Clearly, autobiography is the property neither of conservatives nor of liberals. Giving an account of God's work in one's life as one understands it is called *giving a testimony*. Like giving testimony in court, we recount what we have seen and experienced. That's not all theology is, but it's a great place to begin.

There is a long and rich tradition of "telling one's story" within most Christian denominations, including most of the mainline traditions. In the conservative evangelical world that first formed me as a Christian, we were asked to give our testimony so often that it became a highly formed and nuanced narrative, adaptable to multiple audiences. As a summer missionary in Europe during college, I learned to give my testimony in halting German to small groups of Austrian teenagers who had come to play soccer with us on their local soccer field (or, more accurately, who had just wiped us off the face of the globe with their far superior soccer skills). As a member of the traveling brass choir at Westmont College, I would give my testimony to audiences during the programs we played at various churches. As a youth minister, I learned to adapt the narrative in ways that would inspire the youth to think about their own relationship with Jesus, so that they could learn to tell their own stories.

Testimonies do not need to describe dramatic conversions. Equally acceptable is the testimony that you were born into a Christian family, that you somehow always experienced God in and through the church, and that this has been a quiet, undramatic, yet still central part of your life across many decades. Nor do testimonies have to be church-based. You can give a testimony of your questing for God across many different religious practices and traditions, before finally coming to a deep sense of the presence of the divine in a very private way—without any explicit connection to organized religion whatsoever.

Testimonies always include autobiography, however. They start with simple narratives of our encountering God, coming to know God, seeking to walk with God. In the first chapter of his new book, *Communicating Christianity in the Public Square: A How and Why Guide for Progressive Christians*, Delwin Brown puts it like this:

> When we are called upon to say who we are, we begin, if we are wise, by telling our story. When we are asked what we stand for, we begin by describing the heritage that has formed us. We tell our story not to boast, though sometimes it makes us proud, nor to reject it, though sometimes it causes us shame. We tell of our heritage because it is ours.[2]

Whenever you get confused about what the word *theology* might mean, just go back to this core idea of reciting the narrative of your life before God. It lies at the foundation of everything else that I say. It's a good stepping-off-point, or point of reference, as you engage the more complex parts of the Seven Core Christian Questions.

The glory of testimonies is their simplicity. Telling our own stories is just what we

Theology always starts with reciting the narrative of your life before God.

do as human beings. When we sit in a coffee shop and eavesdrop on the chatter at nearby tables, the talk is almost always in the form of narratives: "Maggie told him that she didn't want to go out with him anymore. Then he was all like, 'But we went to the prom together!' And she was all like, 'But, like, you never called me again after that.'" Or, "I dropped my mom off at the senior citizens' center, then I drove to do my workout and to get my hair done. After that I had to do a little shopping. And then I picked the kids up after school. . . . "

Again, the glory of testimonies is that they are simple; they are the most natural and basic genre we know. Testimonies explain in personal terms why you have come to see your life as bound up inextricably with the love and grace of God. That's something that all of us who believe in God can do—or, if we can't yet, we can learn it pretty quickly. This is Theology 101. If you've never done this, I urge you to put this book down right now, call up a friend, and ask that person to listen while you try telling your own personal testimony for the first time. Or write an email to someone in which you try to do it. (If you don't believe in any God, you're welcome to read on, of course. Perhaps you'll find it helpful to know that *to believe in God* doesn't have to be any more complicated than to have some such story to tell.)

But the *problem* with testimonies is also that they are so simple. Eventually one needs to be able to explain, at least to oneself, why one chose to go to a Christian college rather than a secular college. One needs to be able to say why she goes to a church that is "open and affirming," or why he thinks that "friendship evangelism" is better than street-corner evangelism, or why she thinks that working out or becoming a vegetarian is an important part of her Christian discipleship. The committee has to say why it voted to send church funds to independent mission boards rather than giving through the mission initiatives of its own denomination. In each case one tells one's own story, using the language of God, the life and teaching of Jesus, and the call to discipleship. As the issues get more complicated, the narrative needs to get more complicated as well. Faced with real complexities, we have to dig a bit deeper into our beliefs and the sources of our belief (Scripture, tradition, reason, and experience) in order to explain why we make the decisions we make. That's where the Seven Core Christian Questions—and our answers to them—come into play.

Telling Theological Stories at the Congregational Level— and Beyond

Our structure of congregations has its origin in the Jewish tradition. Traditionally, a Jewish congregation (a *minyan*) was a group of families with at least ten adult males. As it grew in size, a congregation would call a teacher, or rabbi, to teach them Torah and the principles of the observance of Jewish law. The observance of the 613 laws (the *mitzvot*) in Torah has an individual dimension, of course. But it also involves activities of the family at home and of the worshiping and observing congregation. Interpreting Jewish law in the broader sense (*Halakha*), for example, requires the assistance of a trained rabbi who knows the history of commentary and interpretation of what the law requires.

A Christian congregation is a local worshiping community. The most basic principle that underlies it is the statement of Jesus quoted in Matthew, "Where two or three are gathered in my name, I am there among them" (Matt. 18:20). The book of Acts describes the development of congregations in multiple cities, mostly following the narrative of the missionary journeys of Paul. According to Acts 2 and 4, congregations were places where the Lord's Supper was celebrated, where the gospel of Jesus was proclaimed, where people took care of other members of the body of Christ, and from which they reached out to their communities. Gradually, over the course of Paul's life and the years that followed, some of these functions were developed into explicit roles. Among these the New Testament lists teachers, prophets, presbyters, and deacons.

The same framework we explored for individual believers also applies to groups of believers. *A congregation is a place where we come together to tell the corporate narrative of our life together with God,* as well as to observe the rites and liturgies that help us to remember and experience that story. We invite seekers to come and listen and participate as they wish, so that they may be exposed to this narrative and decide whether they wish to make it part of their own stories as well. For us as members, our meeting together allows a corporate dimension to emerge out of the individual dimensions of our various stories. I have elsewhere written much about this emergence.[3] Suffice it to say that one of the great wonders of the natural and social worlds is that new types of phenomena, new forms of behavior, and new instances of self-understanding continually emerge. Parts come together to form wholes greater then themselves. A congregation is a place where, out of the individual stories, a new whole emerges—the corporate narrative of the body of Christ.

This story does not have to be expressed in propositions or set in stone for all time. Just as our individual stories are constantly growing and developing, one expects that the corporate story of a congregation will grow and develop as well. And just as our individual stories are testimonies about God's will and action intersecting with our own lives, so also will our corporate life together be a tale of God's call and action in our midst.

Why is it, then, that we are so hesitant about telling theological stories in our congregations? As my colleagues and I have explored dozens, if not scores, of church websites, we found (to our surprise) that it is relatively rare to find congregations telling their own story. There are exceptions. Brian McLaren's home church, Cedar Ridge Community Church, tells its story in terms of three fundamental categories: discipleship, growth, and community.[4] Community, for example, stretches well beyond the church walls, encompassing grass-roots activity, church-based activity, and neighborhood-based activity. This is simple but powerful.

Nor are theological narratives limited to congregations. Each denomination, Christian organization, and social ministry has its own story to tell, its own testimony to give. The challenge is that there are living narratives and dead narratives. For narratives to remain alive, they must be taken up within the ever-evolving stories of people here and now. Many Lutherans still build Luther's theology of "justification by faith" into their own theologies. But can Presbyterians still affirm the narrative of Calvin's *Institutes* and make it their own? Do Methodists still locate themselves in John Wesley's life and ministry, in his call to Christian perfection, and in the history of Methodist revivals and evangelism? Every Christian organization needs to ground its own call to ministry in the gospel narrative and in responses to the Seven Core Christian Questions. There is no way to achieve this task other than to do the constructive theological work that links the Christian testimony "once given" to the *here and now* of one's own context for ministry.

12. Theologies in Action

Theology starts, I've argued, with exploring the intersections between my story and God's story. It includes bringing to the surface the deep assumptions I've already made about who God is and testing them against the four sources of Scripture, tradition, reason, and experience. It involves coming back again and again to the Seven Core Christian Questions and formulating ever more adequate answers. For Christians, it means continually living before the question, "Who do *you* say that I am?"

I've also contended that all who attempt to follow Jesus' Way already have their own theologies. Some are intellectually more developed, others more intuitive; some are more conscious, others largely subconscious or unconscious. Some are very abstract ("The being and essence of God consists in the following eight features. . . ."), others highly concrete ("I work with homeless people because I am grateful for God's saving grace in my life"). Advocates of different theologies may see things differently. Sometimes they're not sure that "the other guys" are really doing theology at all. (A little more charity on this front would be a good thing.) But they are all producing theologies nonetheless.

That's the start. Now let's go deeper.

Put Your Thought Where Your Heart Is

People today are suspicious of *-ologies*, and Christians are no exception. It almost doesn't matter what letters you put before the dash: immun-ology, Buddh-ology, neur-ology, etym-ology, or the-ology. The suffice *-ology* might originally have meant merely "the study of," but for most readers today it has come to suggest dry, boring, abstract, needlessly complex, and irrelevant to all important real-life concerns.

If theology is to be returned to real-life Christians—female and male, young and old, conservative and liberal—then we must somehow overcome this suspicion about -*ologies*. The quickest way to get there is to think of the -*ology* in "theology" as meaning not "the study of" but just "thinking about." And we should generalize the *theo-* to mean not only God (*theos*), but *every aspect of one's Christian faith*. Whenever you stop to think about what you believe, you are already doing theology. Of course, it appears that some people don't want to think about their faith at all, no matter how broadly we define the word. As you can see, I'm trying to make you dissatisfied with that response. I'm urging every Christian to be a life-long thinker, *especially when it comes to faith*. I'm hoping to help pack the churches with people who ask hard questions and won't rest satisfied until they find real answers. Then, I trust, they'll put feet on their beliefs and start to transform their churches and the society around them!

"But what if people really don't want to think about their faith?" you ask. Do you mean the faith in God that (they say) lies at the very center of their life, that guides them in their most important decisions, that supplies meaning to all that they do, that helps them understand the past of this universe, the present of the world situation, and the future eternity in which they stake their hopes? "Yes, that one. What can one do when people don't want to think about their faith?"

Well, maybe an analogy will help. I took up tennis in mid-life. Now if you know anything about tennis, you know that people who don't start early are likely to be "duffers" to their dying day. (Indeed, it's likely that their dying day will occur on a tennis court as they rush for a ball they'll never reach.) But that doesn't stop me from being immensely passionate about tennis—thinking about it constantly, reading books, and taking my lessons with Allison, the club pro, so seriously that you'd think I was preparing for a Grand Slam tournament.

Nor am I alone. Even the grayest and the most out-of-shape-looking players talk incessantly about winning strategies, "the mental game," and the most recent matches at the French Open. Even the guys at the bottom of the singles' ladder go on and on about their concept of how to hit a serve or how to psych out the other player (mostly just psyching out themselves in the process). You get the point: these are not great players or highly trained theorists of the game. It's just that they're passionate about their sport, so how can they help but talk about it all the time?

Okay, that's tennis. But if we are passionate about our Christian faith, wouldn't we expect *at least* as much reflection and reading and talk about who it is we believe in, how that helps us interpret the contemporary world, and how to communicate these ideas effectively to other persons? So if we participate in or visit a church community where no one talks about his or her faith—which happens more often than one would expect—we ought to start looking for explanations. Why the resounding silence? After all, it's human nature to talk about what we care about most. Moms and dads talk about their kids; computer programmers talk about programming languages; movie fans talk incessantly about films; musicians are always talking about music—you can extend the list at will.

So something is wrong here. If we're going to change it, we have to first understand it. Here are the five most likely possibilities:

1. The folks in this church don't really believe anything. They're here out of habit or a sense of obligation or for social respectability or because it feels good to sit through a service and to sing the hymns.

2. The folks in the pews do share some beliefs and values in common, but it's not distinctively *Christian* beliefs and values that make them a community. Maybe similarities in their race, age, class, financial status, family values, or political beliefs are the magnet that draws them together.

3. People hold deep Christian convictions but somehow feel that it's not appropriate to talk about them. Perhaps they worry that they would seem too intellectual, or hypocritical, or too gung-ho about their faith if they talked about it a lot.

4. Perhaps these people no longer know *what* to believe. Perhaps they have more questions than answers. They might care deeply about what it means to be a Jesus follower and how to interpret the world from that standpoint, but they no longer know what a deep Christian identity means in today's world—at least, what it means *for them*. (I actually think this is true in many, many churches today.)

5. Perhaps none of the above is true. It could be that in this church, as in many churches, there just aren't the right kinds of meetings or occasions or discussion groups where people are encouraged to

ask questions and to formulate what they really believe. Perhaps it doesn't feel safe to be so honest. I think a lot of people *wish* that their Sunday morning experience was deeper, more profound, more meaningful. But many find that Sunday mornings aren't structured in a way that allows them to have the conversations and connections for which they yearn.

The situation tends to be easier to change as we move down the list. (The first two present the biggest challenges.) But how can we decide which of these options, if any, is true in a given church?

Try This Experiment in Your Local Church

Here's an experiment to try out in your local church, or in a congregation that you might visit. Wander through the crowd during church coffee hour and listen in on the conversations as you walk by. If I'm correct in thinking that people talk about what really matters to them, what you hear should help you determine the values and concerns that tie this particular group of people together, that make them into a community at this place and time. And if you listen very carefully, sometimes you can hear what's *not* being said.

If you want, you can take the experiment deeper by attending one or more church committee meetings as a visitor. (Usually committees are only too happy to have someone visit since, as you might suspect, not a lot of people do this voluntarily.) Listen closely to the topics of conversation. Most of all, listen to the reasons people give when they reach a decision. What factors do leaders appeal to when they justify their decisions and actions? What dominates: considerations of expediency, or pragmatic effectiveness, or tradition ("it's *always* been done this way!"), or respectability, or what? Usually decisions reflect some set of shared values, though these are often left implicit and unstated. What shared values are being expressed?

Of particular interest is how Scripture is used in decision making (if it's used at all). Are verses by themselves treated as the final authority that legitimizes specific decisions? Are they read as examples, as models, as metaphors, as anecdotes, or as direct recipes for action? Are they cited as commonsense wisdom, the way we use phrases like, "a stitch in time saves nine" or "a bird in the hand is worth two in the bush" or "it's bad luck to walk under a ladder"? When a biblical story, character, or parable is cited, do speakers assume that its relevance to the contemporary context is obvious, or do they pause to draw out the connections? Are people able to vocalize the assumptions they use when they apply Scripture (or church law) to an actual situation?

Theology means *moving from Scripture and tradition, by means of reason and experience, to application in the contemporary world.* To do it well, we have to get the underlying assumptions out on the table, clarify them, and then use them in making our decisions. We have to agree on our context or contexts. Then we can turn back to Scripture and tradition in light of the results and seek to interpret them anew. At that point we can take these new results and use them as a clearer lens through which to read today's world and our own calling in it. We do discipleship and ministry in light of our emerging understand-

> Theology means moving from Scripture and tradition, by means of reason and experience, to application in the world.

ing. With that experience in hand, we go back *again* to the original texts and the inherited beliefs. Back and forth and back and forth. Theology is just this circle.

 ## Don't Sweat the Small Stuff

Richard Carlson's beautiful little book, *Don't Sweat the Small Stuff . . . and it's all small stuff* begins with the statement, "Often we allow ourselves to get all worked up about things that, upon closer examination, *aren't* really that big a deal."[1] It's fantastic advice that Christians also need to hear. We're only going to produce (and live by) transformative theologies when we learn to do a better job with difference within the church.

The reason is simple: under the "big tent" of Christian discipleship is assembled a vast group of very, very different people. Our cultures, races, and languages vary; our childhoods, educations, and indoctrinations vary; our prejudices and life experiences vary. Add to that a vast host of individual foibles and idiosyncrasies (oh, did you say you don't have any?). Now remember that it's human nature not to like those who are different. We tend to be suspicious of those who aren't like us—in age or appearance or background. We tend to not associate with people who don't look like us, or who come from a different part of the country (or world), or who use language differently. The results of these natural human tendencies have been disastrous for the church. *The continual war to show that our group is right, and to marginalize those who differ from us, in the end diminishes all of us. It undercuts not only what is good in others' work but also what is good in our own.* In the end this attitude threatens to destroy the church as the body of those who together seek to follow Christ.

Judging from church history, this has always been a very hard lesson for folks to grasp. From the beginning to our own day, church leaders have disparaged those with whom they disagree, doubted their sincerity as disciples, and condemned others based on their own (sometimes narrow) understanding of orthodoxy. Too easily the words fall from our lips: "What God *most* desires is. . . . "—and then we list our own strongest concerns. Or we proclaim, "But certain actions, and especially. . . . "—and here we add the sin that *we* are most concerned about—"are sins in God's eyes," and we declare, "We simply must hold the line for the sake of the purity of the church and the purity of the gospel!" Of course, we *could* be right about the phrases that we add into these sentences. The trouble is, we might be wrong as well. Predictably, we are much better at identifying the speck of sin in our neighbor's eye, and less good at identifying the logs of sin in our own (Matt. 7:3). Achieving the humility that it takes to say this is the starting point. Without it we will never achieve any powerful common voice either as church or as Christians in society.

Perhaps someone will object that I'm being "soft on sin." Not at all. But I want to be *hardest* on sin when it comes to my own sins. It's our insistence on talking so loudly about the failures of others—whether theological or moral—that most hurts the perception of Christians within our society. Consider what our various disputes look like to those who have always stood outside the church as observers, to those who have recently left, or to those who are about to do so. Can't you hear what they are saying: You squabble endlessly over what appear to us to be trivial issues. You fiddle while Rome burns. You are better at condemning each other than you are at seeking to manifest together the common calling of Christian discipleship. You seem more interested in turf-protection than in taking on the urgent challenges of our day. Too often you are prepared "to strain out a gnat and swallow a camel" (a phrase that Jesus preceded with, "You blind guides!" Matt. 23:24). In this way you appear rather different from your own Teacher, Jesus, who was somehow able to rise above the squabbles of his day and to continually turn people's attention back to the really fundamental questions: the importance of love, of compassion, of forgiveness, of repentance, of community. The more you fight for your own purity and your own causes, the less we see in you the One whom you are trying to reflect and emulate!

One reason to make our theology explicit is to keep us focused on the central issues. Some of the issues that the churches are now debating are indeed important. But are they all? Remember, we are also accountable for what we omit, for what we fail to say, for what gets obscured in the midst of our various public disputes. Somehow this didn't happen with Jesus:

> Keeping a close watch on him, they sent spies, who pretended to be honest. They hoped to catch Jesus in something he said so that they might hand him over to the power and authority of the governor. So the spies questioned him: "Teacher, we know that you speak and teach what is right, and that you do not show partiality but teach the way of God in accordance with the truth. Is it right for us to pay taxes to Caesar or not?"
>
> He saw through their duplicity and said to them, "Show me a denarius. Whose portrait and inscription are on it?"
>
> "Caesar's," they replied.
>
> He said to them, "Then give to Caesar what is Caesar's, and to God what is God's."
>
> They were unable to trap him in what he had said there in public. And astonished by his answer, they became silent. (Luke 20:20-26, NIV)

 ## Viewing Theologies as Complementary, Not Mutually Exclusive

Our squabbles sometimes remind me of the famous story of the four blind men and the elephant. Each one touches the part that's closest to him and assumes that the whole is just like his particular part: tusk, trunk, leg, tail. In fact, there are whole branches of the church that specialize in one or another theological emphasis. The trouble is that each branch proclaims its particular strengths and insights—and then proceeds to dismiss what everyone else does as unnecessary, inferior, or just plain wrong.

It's time for us to start building bridges rather than staking out one hostile terrain or another. Consider for a moment the various strengths of the different branches of Christianity. Look what happens when we don't view them as combating forces but as complementary resources for a richer Christian response to today's world:

1. Some persons, congregations, and denominations have a deep commitment to a close reading of Scripture. Their high view of biblical inspiration leads them to careful study of individual authors. They know how to build gradually from textual study to (say) a theology of the gospels or a Pauline theology, then to a New Testament theology, and finally to a rich and sophisticated biblical theology as the grounds for a systematic presentation of Christian belief. (I think of evangelicals and conservatives as having particular strengths in these areas.)

2. Others combine these strengths with high respect for and close study of the classic creeds and theologians: the Patristic theologians, the Cappadocian Fathers, Augustine, medieval and Reformation thinkers, to name a few. These individuals and groups are gifted at mining the resources of the past in order to guide the church in the present. In recent years, for example, I've learned an immense amount from members of the Eastern Orthodox churches, who are steeped in the early centuries of Christian history more than perhaps any other branch of the church today.

3. Still others specialize in the language and concerns of today's world. They understand contemporary social and political issues at a very deep level, and they can communicate them to us in such a way that we experience them as calls to Christian action. The expertise of these individuals and groups lies in recognizing the social wrongs and injustices to which Christians should be giving a prophetic response. (These tendencies tend to be more pronounced among people who are called liberals or progressives.)

4. Finally, there are those who are skilled at expressing the distinctive features of modern thought or the challenges of contemporary science or the world-and-life-views of other religious traditions. Their particular gift lies in helping the church to gain more insight into the world around us. (Let's call them the scholars.)

When they are presented in this way, without the negative rhetoric, it's easy to see that the four categories can be viewed as complementary. Can you imagine the church that could emerge when all these strengths are honored and used? Christian voices become strongest and clearest when all four work as allies. We're able to speak prophetically to contemporary injustices and dilemmas, yet we do so based on the distinctive features of our Scriptures and historical tradition. I call it *from roots to relevance*: discovering the powerful insights the Christian tradition has to offer when it is interpreted and applied to the contemporary world. Uncovering these connections is the heart and soul of Christian theology.

13. A Theology of Self-Emptying
for the Church

Theologies always involve the weaving together of God's story and one or more human stories. In Christian theologies, Jesus' life and teaching play a central role in the resulting narrative. We've explored in more general terms what theologies are and aren't. It's time now to consider a very specific example of how a theology is discovered, constructed, and applied. Given all I've said, I have no choice but to keep it personal. The theology you're about to read is also my theology.

The idea is simple: we have been talking about the Seven Core Christian Questions. These are the questions to which, in one form or another, the Christian church has come back again and again. When I ask future pastors to prepare their Credos, their statements of faith, I ask them to give sophisticated responses to each of these seven questions:

- Who is God, and how is God related to the world? (the doctrine of God and the God-world relation)
- Who is Jesus Christ? What was his life, teaching, and mission? (christology)
- Who is the Holy Spirit? How is the Spirit related to the Father and to the Son (the question of the Trinity)? (pneumatology)
- What is humanity, man and woman? How are we like the other animals, and what is the "image of God" that distinguishes us from other animals? (anthropology)
- What and why is sin? What is salvation? What is Jesus' role in bringing it about, and what is our role? How is salvation linked to discipleship and sanctification? (soteriology)
- What is the church? (ecclesiology) (It's only a four-word question, but there is much, much to be said here.)

- What is the Christian hope? What occurs after death, and what is heaven? And what is the role of Jesus Christ in this all? (eschatology)

One must also pay attention to the roles played by all four of the different *sources* of theology in answering each of these questions for him- or herself:

- What does Scripture teach? How does it help us to answer each question?
- What has the Christian tradition held? What must be retained and what may have been mistaken in the traditional answers that were given to these questions?
- What role does reason play? (This might include science, philosophy, other academic disciplines, and other world religious traditions.)
- What role does experience play—both individual experience and the corporate experience of the church—in answering each question?

There is no briefer, clearer account of the emerging theologies of our day than Doug Pagitt's *The Emerging Church and Embodied Theology*. In fact, Doug's assumptions about theology are so insightful that I repeat them here, as a sort of test for the reflections that you'll be reading in a moment. Among his guidelines are:

- Theology is meant to be temporary
- Theology is meant to be profession
- Theology is always contextual
- Theology is to be particular
- Theology is a Spirit-led practice
- Our theology is taking place in an age of tremendous change
- Theology is for unity, not uniformity
- Theology is to be participatory
- Christendom is not the goal[1]

One caution: this experiment will only really work if you read it side by side with other theologies. If you take my example as the *only* framework for a genuinely transforming theology today, it would invalidate the entire message of this book. Ideally I would write a chapter each on four or five *different* practical theologies for our day, in order to encourage you to develop your own Credo, your own statement of belief. There's not enough space to do that here. But the least I can do is to encourage you to read some of the other great new theologies that are being written. Read a post-conservative theologian like Roger Olson. Read a clear process theologian like John Cobb, or Marjorie Suchocki's *God, Christ, Church* (Crossroad, 1992). Read the theological reflections of an emergent thinker like Brian McLaren. Read Scot McKnight's *A Community Called Atonement* (Abingdon, 2007), where Scot (in the final part) interprets atonement as a form of *praxis*, as something we actually do in the world. In his account atonement as "missional praxis" takes on many forms: fellowship, justice, baptism, Eucharist, and prayer, to name a few.

When I work with church groups and with future pastors, I caution them that theology is never done from some abstract place. A theology is never "a view from nowhere." Thus they must begin as concretely as possible. I begin with the ancient Christian hymn, quoted by Paul in Philippians 2, as my starting point, but I expect and urge others to begin in different places. Begin from where you live. If you are called to ministry with youth, or with Twelve-Step programs, or with migrant workers, or with mixed-race congregations, or with the aging, you *should* bring the context and concerns of your ministry to your emerging theology. If you are nursing a sick relative, or had a parent die, or have gone through a divorce, or lost your job, that context should play a role in how you answer the Seven Core Christian Questions. If you are a professional scientist, you will have different concerns from those of a business woman, a school teacher, a denominational administrator, or a church musician.

One final thought: people often say that you cannot tell part of the Christian story unless you tell the whole Christian story. I agree that the church as a whole needs to make known the entire Christian proclamation, but I do not agree that every Christian who struggles to find his or her own distinctive voice must always tell the whole story every time. That's a recipe for silence (which is in fact what has happened!) The reason is that, to meet this standard, you'd have to take *yourself* out of the equation. If you speak from the heart about your particular Christian location, then you will inevitably emphasize the things that *you* have known and understood and experienced. There is an honesty and authenticity about such first-person experience that, in my experience, speaks volumes. So let the reader beware:

there is much more to Christian proclamation than my story, as there is more to Paul than Philippians, more to Philippians than the passage about Jesus' self-emptying, and more even to this specific passage than the verses on which I focus.

The Christ Hymn in Philippians 2

"Have this mind among yourselves, which you have in Christ Jesus. . . ." (Phil. 2:5, RSV) What you're about to read is, from a Christian perspective, *the* central narrative in God's relationship with the world God created. The particular contribution of Christian voices within the dialogue of world religions is to talk about this narrative. We believe that the values embodied here offer a crucial window onto the divine nature and purposes. In fact, for us it is *the central window.*

Thus it's all the more interesting that Paul begins the passage by calling us not to hold the narrative at arm's length. It must not be placed up in the heavens, out there somewhere, or shoved away onto a distant holy altar, or left to rest somewhere in ancient history. He wants it to represent the "mind" that we have about Christianity. The Greek word is *phroneisthō,* which means "be minded in this way." It's interesting that the root for this word is *phronesis,* which is the word that the Greek philosopher Aristotle uses for practical wisdom—that down-to-earth sort of wisdom people live by when they are good at dealing with things and people in the actual world. Paul also emphasizes that this is not just a story about the eternal deity, but it reflects the very practical way of thinking that Jesus manifested in his earthly life. And it is that mind-set that Jesus lived that we are to have in our own daily living.

". . . who, though he was in the form of God, did not count equality with God a thing to be grasped" (v. 6). Here Paul gives the background to what Christians call the incarnation, the becoming human of God. The Jesus whose "mind" we are to emulate was, before his birth, in the very form of God and enjoyed "equality with God." Although Paul does not engage here in any lofty speculations as to how this could be, this is the position that the church later came to describe in the doctrine of the Trinity—the belief that the one divine Godhead is actually constituted by three "persons" (or aspects—*hypostases*).

Now I must admit that, when I am working to interweave my story with God's story, I do not pause for long to speculate on how there could be a pre-incarnate logos or what it means in technical terms for Jesus Christ to be God, the second person of the Trinity. I fear we theologians may have over-emphasized these questions, forcing them on others too early and without enough sensitivity. Telling my story does not require me to legislate these doctrines for the church community as a whole.[2] My story is so small and humble that it can get by with far less nuanced observations. This Jesus, whose "mind" I am being called to emulate, was no ordinary mortal. His life was tied up in some mysterious way with the very life of God. Whatever "equality with God" may mean, it certainly means that this is an extremely authoritative story for those of us who interpret our lives in terms of it. The text tells me that there must be something distinctive about Jesus' life, if he was "in the form of God."

Finally, the shocking phrase, "did not count equality with God *something to be grasped*," deserves special attention. It suggests a distinction between those who "grasp" at equality with God, and those who, like Christ Jesus, do not grasp at (or for) this equality. It has never crossed my mind to grasp at equality with God; my grasping is of a much more petty nature: grasping for power or prestige or honor. Still, the verse tells me that my theology will have to include some crucial categories that caution me about grasping. And it will have to mention the sorts of things that I and those around me tend to grasp at: money and wealth; power and prestige; influence; control over others; and the like.

". . . *but emptied himself. . .* " (v. 7). Here the Greek verb is *ekenōsen* from the noun *kenosis*, for self-emptying. Theologians thus call this the "kenotic" hymn, and the technical name for the theology I am putting forward is *kenotic theology*.

In this notion of self-emptying we encounter what is for me the central Christian teaching about Jesus' "mind," about God's self-revelation—and indeed about God's own eternal nature. When I ask what it means for me to try to love as God loves, the answer must always begin with self-emptying. What Christ emptied himself of was having the *highest conceivable* glory, the glory of equality with God's eternal nature. I suspect that for most of us the temptations are rather more humble. Still, the text forewarns me to pay attention to the temptations that I am inclined to grasp at and not let go.

I expect that these will include possessions, lifestyles, social relationships, privileges, longings and lusts, pride, and matters of belief. That is, I expect to find that the grasping will involve holding onto private prejudices, assumptions, or inherited systems of belief, *including my religious beliefs, my beliefs about God and ultimate values.*

If a theology and the lifestyle that goes with it are to be Christ-like, they will be pervaded by this self-emptying. They will involve letting go of the security and neatness of systems of belief that produce pride. I must be careful not to hold things or beliefs as if they were my right or the ground of my personal security, safety, and identity. From the text I expect to find this need for self-emptying lying at the very core of my being, beliefs, and desires—there where it matters most, and there where I find it hardest to recognize.

". . . taking the form of a servant, being born in the likeness of men . . ." (v. 7). This ancient Christian hymn, which we believe is the oldest Christian hymn found in the New Testament (not including the baptismal formula in Matt. 28:18-20), cites two examples of what Christ empties himself to become: "a servant," and "the likeness of men." Clearly, for God to become a human being was a huge form of humbling; we are, after all, rather tiny and limited creatures. You don't even need the notion of God in order to recognize how limited we are. Imagine what humanity and this planet would be like if every human had the genius of Einstein, or the spiritual vision of Ghandi. Now imagine that every human being, or even a significant number of us, had even twice Einstein's intelligence. Instead of being so short-sighted, for example, I imagine that we'd be voting for policies that ensured the long-term good of our species, other species, and our planet as a whole. Now imagine that many of us had ten times that intelligence—just think of what we could do! And yet none of this is even a ripple on the chart of divine intelligence, for God's intelligence must be *infinitely* greater than that of an Einstein. Given the contrast, the enormity of Christ's self-emptying begins to sink in.

But Jesus' self-emptying lay not just in becoming human. Of all the types of human he could have become: king, emperor, Mozart, Einstein—he took on the "form of a servant." When I read these words, I hear resonances and echoes of much of the New Testament. I hear the words, "Whoever wants to be first must be the last of all and the servant of all" (Mk. 9:35). I hear the powerful words of Jesus' action just prior to his final supper with his disciples: "Jesus, knowing that the Father had given all things into his hands, and that he had come from God and was going to God, got up from the table, took off his outer robe, and tied a towel around himself. Then he poured water into a basin and began to wash the disciples' feet and to wipe them with the towel that was tied around him" (John 13:3-5).

"And being found in human form he humbled himself and became obedient unto death, even death on a cross" (v. 8). Well before we are adults, we know what death is. We recognize it as the end of all of our projects—that line in the sand after which we no longer lead and decide. It is also the frightful and frightening mystery of the apparent end of all that we have become.

I was a young teenager when my father came home from the hospital after undergoing a brain scan for a tumor that we knew might be terminal. As an atheist, my father was quite certain that there was no life beyond death. He sat on the couch and stared at the floor. After awhile he said aloud, more to himself than to his family who was gathered in the room, "What is death? It is the absolute end. All goes dark. You have no more experiences, no more thoughts or feelings. Everything stops; you are no more."

Because death appears to have this finality, we understand how the greatest possible act of self-sacrifice is to die for another. "No one has greater love than this, to lay down one's life for one's friends" (John 15:13), Jesus said shortly after washing his disciples' feet. There are also better and worse ways to die. As you probably already know, dying on a cross was a particularly gruesome way to die. I will skip over the details; they have already been described in far too much detail in books such as *The Day Christ Died* by Jim Bishop and in movies such as Mel Gibson's *The Passion of the Christ*. The text explicitly mentions "even death on a cross," emphasizing that it is not only the *being dead* that marked Christ's self-emptying, but also the process of being willing to die in such a painful way.

 ## Living the Christ Hymn

That, in short, is the narrative of the Christ. Christians believe that it is at the same time God's story. What does it mean for it to become *my* narrative as well? In some ways that is the central question of this entire book. So I challenge you to try to tell your story, in all the rich and personal detail of an autobiography, *inside of* this story of Jesus' self-emptying. You can meditate directly on the text, as I have done here. You can read it in the broader context of Paul's letter to the Philippians, or the Pauline epistles, or the New Testament, or the Bible as a whole. Indeed, you can stretch your horizons even wider (after all, when the topic is God, nothing that exists really falls completely outside the narrative). Thus you can even read this christological hymn in light of the whole of human history, or the whole history of our earth, or even the whole history of the universe as science is now revealing it to us. You can include other religions or philosophies, or art and literature, or personal experience and psychology. In short, the sky's the limit. *Anything and everything you say as you carry out this exercise is theology.*

> *Learn to tell your story inside the story of Jesus' self-emptying.*

But remember: the results must continue to have something to do with your own life. They have to involve how you follow this Way that Jesus taught and lived. The only way for me to remain true to this insight in what follows is to write from my own perspective. It's not that my perspective is particularly interesting or notable. But, for obvious reasons, it's the only story that I can tell in an authentic manner. (I cannot take credit for your virtues or feel penance for your vices, but I can do so for mine.) If reading about the demands that Christ's self-emptying make on me inspires you to think about what they might mean for you, and thus to begin to do theology in your own right, these next few pages will have served their function.

Recognizing the Faces of Power and Prejudice

I start not overseas, nor with general problems of the world, but with my own contexts. For example, what forms of power do I experience as a male in my society? Numerous studies show that already at the kindergarten level, boy students tend to capture more of the teacher's attention. Teachers tend to give them more air time. According to the research, this pattern continues through elementary and high school and on into college. We know well that, although more positions are now opening up to women, women less frequently receive the highest positions in firms and in government and are often paid less for the same position and work. Thus I know that, when I speak or raise my hand, or when I push forward to get the attention of a salesperson, I am likely to be acknowledged more quickly than the women around me. Add to that a few other social advantages—being tall and deep-voiced and slightly graying—and you have a recipe for preferential treatment.

How should knowing these things affect my discipleship? Christ's self-emptying is clearly relevant. The One whom I follow continually put himself on the side of the outcast, the despised, and the powerless. He warned that those who are well off and who have much in this life "have received their reward" (Matt. 6:16), whereas those who have been cast down will be lifted up. "Blessed are you when people hate you, and when they exclude you, revile you, and defame you on account of the Son of Man. Rejoice in that day and leap for joy, for surely your reward is great in heaven; for that is what their ancestors did to the prophets" (Luke 6:22-23).

The picture of Jesus conveyed so clearly in the Gospels is of one who declined positions of power and prestige to side with the poor and the outcast. His God is the God of Mary's Magnificat: "He has brought down the powerful from their thrones, and lifted up the lowly; he has filled the hungry with good things, and sent the rich away empty" (Luke 1:52-53). The list of the outcasts with whom he associated is almost as long as the Gospels: Mary Magdalene, the Samaritan woman (John 4), the woman caught in adultery (John 8:1-11), the leper, the demon-possessed man, the blind man at Bethsaida (Mark 8: 22-26), or the man who had been blind from birth (Jn. 9). Others are powerful people who stepped out of their powerful positions to come humbly before Jesus, such as the Centurion (Matt. 8:5-13), Zacchaeus the tax collector (Luke 19), and Nicodemus the Pharisee (John 3). Others are characters in Jesus' parables who have become famous examples of his concern for the outcast, such as the beggar Lazarus (Luke 16:20-27) or the man whom the Good Samaritan helped (Luke 10:25-37). One could do an entire Bible study or sermon series based on Jesus' association with outcasts using these and the other examples.

The Jesus of the Gospels focused continually on the same revolutionary transformation: lifting up the humble, and bringing down the powerful. In the Gospels, the kingdom of God is *defined* in terms of this reversal. If I am to be his follower, if I am to be on his side, then I must actively participate in reversing patterns of power and prestige. Exactly how to do this is not always clear; presumably it will vary in different times and places. All I know is that it must begin at home, with me, and not with others elsewhere. Your list may look very different, but here's the beginning of mine:

- I recognize that my wife has been socialized to give, even as I have been socialized to receive from women. It must be my daily practice to begin to reverse this process. I must find ways to give more deeply rather than expecting to receive. Together, we must change our expectations and patterns, so that more of the burden falls on my shoulders and less on hers.

- I can help to reverse the patterns in my teaching and preaching. When in lectures I refer to a doctor or lawyer or hero using "she" instead of "he," I see that it surprises students; they were expecting it to be a man. Even this small step of using "she" as the generic pronoun stops people short, helping to reverse expectations. It helps when the stories of great human achievements often include women; and the stories of human failings must also include males.

- In many groups males are primarily in power. I can help to change this. I can also watch for the tendency of male leaders to implicitly give advantages to other males.

These small steps are only a beginning. That's why I need to move up to the level of theology. Instead of thinking only of individual examples, I need to understand the theological principles, since they extend across life as a whole.

What of race? Racism is inbuilt in human biology and socialization; we are naturally suspicious of those who are different from us. In some ways, racism and sexism are built into us at equally deep levels. The practice of self-emptying means starting the search for signs of inbred racism and sexism *within myself*. It takes some honesty, and the results are not always pretty. If you are a middle-aged, white male and your younger, black female colleague begins to speak, can you notice that your ears hear her words in a different way than they hear that silver-haired, powerful, white male colleague when he speaks? We humans can retrain our ears successfully, but it doesn't happen automatically; we have to do some work to get there. (Similar prejudices slip in, by the way, when the speaker is older or young, or when she comes from a different country, or when he's sitting in a wheelchair.)

I began working on this lesson some years ago by observing my responses to a younger colleague who was a black woman. To check myself, I imagined transcribing her comments as she spoke and then reading them from a piece of paper. Then I tried the same experiment with the white, silver-haired, senior colleague as he spoke. Then I mentally compared the two documents in my head. The result was an eye-opener: her comments were more coherent, more complex, analytically deeper, and more to the point than were his. But that's not what my ears had been telling me. I had to start dealing with the attitudes in my head that were skewing my hearing.

There are dozens of similar exercises that many of us need to practice as part of our ongoing training in self-emptying. My list includes:

- Am I calling on the women in my classes as frequently as the men?
- Am I helping the students to overcome their own implicit sexism and racism?
- Am I being honest with others about my own weaknesses, so that they can hold me accountable?
- Am I selfishly taking advantage of the opportunities that are handed to me as a white male? Or am I helping to make the playing field more equal?

Do you know what your most urgent lessons are? Theology, if it is to be honest, must begin with one's own temptations and weaknesses. Any theological reflection that lifts up a person when he actually requires some self-emptying is not in the spirit of the one who "humbled himself and became obedient unto death." Each of us needs to begin with the areas in which he or she is most likely to be weak and most tempted to act in a non-Christ-like manner.

Perhaps you noticed that my reading of Philippians 2 only went as far as verse 8. I did not discuss the last three verses: "Therefore God has highly exalted him and bestowed on him the name which is above every name, that at the name of Jesus every knee should bow, in heaven and on earth and under the earth, and every tongue confess that Jesus Christ is Lord, to the glory of God the Father" (Phil. 2: 9-11 RSV). These verses remain part of the Christian tradition, of course. But stressing my future exaltation is not the way for me to do theology authentically. The lesson to which *I* am led is a different one: "From everyone to whom much has been given, much will be required; and from the one to whom much has been entrusted, even more will be demanded" (Luke 12:48).

By contrast, many women do *not* need to start with the call to self-emptying. A woman's need might well be the opposite: to achieve a stronger sense of self and self-confidence. Similarly, people who are oppressed by society usually don't need to begin by humbling themselves. Their first need may be to achieve the basic rights and privileges that others of us already enjoy—and the sense of deserving just treatment within society. Of course, I don't believe that being the most oppressed makes one perfect either! People on the bottom rungs of our society's ladder also have areas where they need to grow and become better disciples. But it's not up to the privileged among us to tell *them* what those areas are.

In short, the calling for each of us, and hence the starting point for each one's theology, must begin with the lessons that *he or she* needs to learn. Remember that great passage on this topic in The Chronicles of Narnia by C.S. Lewis? In the penultimate chapter of *The Horse and His Boy*, the heroine Aravis finally meets Aslan, and he tells her what he has done to and for her during her journey. She is worried about what will happen to the servant-girl she left behind, but Aslan responds, "Child, I am telling you your story, not hers. No one is told any story but their own."[3] (If you're a Narnia fan, you'll know that, when Shasta meets Aslan for the first time in the same book, Aslan says almost identical words to him as well.) We need to work harder at hearing, and then telling, our own story.

 ## Self-Emptying in Christian Congregations

The practice of self-emptying is not a purely private affair. Structures of power become more noticeable, and more invidious, as one moves to broader and broader social structures. Sadly, congregations can also be a primary location for unjust and unhealthy social practices. Just as each disciple must look for hypocrisy and blind spots before God, so also must each congregation. And, as with individuals, the questions and the answers will not be identical:

- Do we give more attention to the prestigious members and visitors—those who are attractive or well-dressed or well-spoken?

- Do those of us who naturally receive the best treatment begin to take this for granted, and are we among those who make it more difficult to produce change?
- Do the pastors and visible leaders get the honor in our congregation, whereas the deacons and others become (relatively speaking) invisible?
- Do we practice "the priesthood of all believers," or do only the ordained clergy really count?
- Do we spend most of our money and time on ourselves? Are our concerns narrow, or are they as broad as the kingdom of God?

Just as we must admit our personal tendencies toward racism and sexism, so also we as congregations must confess to the same thing. Whoever would be first among us must become last of all and a servant to all. It is a natural human tendency to honor our leaders and give them the most prestige and the greatest benefits. When *we* become leaders, it's equally natural to allow, and even to expect, the same adoration and honor—as it says on the college diploma, "With all the rights and privileges pertaining thereunto." Imagine what would it look like to construct a topsy-turvy congregation, a congregation that manifested the "Great Reversal" that Jesus preached. It would be a powerful community in which to participate. (Or would we have a hard time being part of such a place?)

I remember the first time I heard the letters "NOCD." They came from the mouth of a deacon in a liberally inclined Presbyterian church, a woman who was active in ministry with the Hispanic community in her town, a person with solid progressive credentials. Thus it surprised me that she would warn her daughter away from friendship with certain people, giving as her reason that they are "Not Our Class, Dear." I was even more surprised that she did not perceive any conflict whatsoever between her involvement in social justice ministries and this inclination to divide the world up into distinct classes, with her and her family inhabiting the upper class. I remember feeling equal surprise when a member of a similar church spoke of the black children on the street as "picaninnies"—a term she *never* used of white children. *We are usually blind to in-group/out-group thinking.*

If we're honest, we have to admit to the tendency to hang out with those who are most like ourselves. Recognizing this natural tendency to seek out those with whom we are most comfortable is the first step. For example, it allows a church to consciously construct activities, programs, and encounters that take people outside their comfort zone. In fact, there are a wide variety of steps that groups can take, depending on how far along a given congregation and its members are (or, conversely, how deeply dominated they are by in-group versus out-group thinking). These steps include:

- organizing discussion groups or Bible studies or church dinners that pair church members with others with whom they do not normally speak or socialize;
- organizing discussions that bring to the surface social and political and theological differences, teaching people how to understand and listen to the other;
- inviting guest speakers who teach on hearing difference, conflict resolution, integration, racism, and so forth;
- arranging programs of outreach into one's neighborhood, which often involves inviting people into the congregation who are "not like us;"
- inviting speakers from churches whose theology is different from one's own, in order to practice listening and understanding what motivates their beliefs;
- inviting speakers from other religious traditions, with the same goal;
- inviting speakers who hold theological positions that are disturbing to members of one's own congregation. It is sometimes easier to listen to a visiting rabbi or Buddhist monk than it is for opponents of gay ordination to hear its defenders (or, for that matter, defenders of gay ordination to listen to its opponents.)

Like other human and theological dilemmas (the old faith-versus-works dilemma comes to mind), each group and congregation has to find its own balance in practice. There's no way around it: sometimes humans need their creature comforts. Churches are no exception. Most of us are unable to push ourselves too far in the direction of self-emptying without becoming neurotic in the process. All of us know some individuals who are deeply and almost continually self-giving. But most normal humans can keep giving only for so long before we begin to experience what the technical literature calls "compassion fatigue." We feel as though we simply have nothing else to give. Those who go on giving anyway often become insincere or neurotic. Pastors are no exception: those who continue self-sacrificing until there's nothing left sooner or later find themselves unable to function any longer—and then everyone wonders why they suddenly gave up professional ministry!

The same is true of congregations. Whether one approves of it or not, there's a pretty deep human need sometimes just to hang out with people who are like us. Every healthy congregation has to provide sufficient opportunities for this to happen. The need is equally strong for youth groups and senior citizens' groups, for small congregations and large ones, for conservatives and for progressives. I remember once pushing a congregation too hard in the direction of integration with the "marginalized others" in our community, until I had a virtual rebellion on my hands. If you push too hard, people simply don't want to come any longer. Finding the right balance is a matter of good leadership; no book will teach you exactly how to find it.[4]

Uniting Proclamation with Self-Emptying

Some of us only know a triumphal form of Christian proclamation. In the very conservative world of my high school years, for example, we were certain that we had the one and only truth, and we proclaimed it as such. The people we talked to, we believed, were lost in their sins and faced damnation. We sang that great old Christian hymn, "Amazing grace, how sweet the sound, that saved a wretch like me." We knew that the people we approched were wretches themselves, except that (unlike us) they lacked the amazing grace. God could work through us, because we had the Holy Spirit, and we were washed as white as snow. But we were a bit more skeptical whether the others could ever really make it. We felt the same about all other religions, all philosophies, and all science; they were "hollow and deceptive philosophy, which depends on human tradition and the basic principles of this world"(Col. 2:8, NIV). I remember well the summer I spent after high school trying to decide whether it was okay even to read any books other than the Bible (and I cringe as I think of it). Unmovable in our certainty, we knew that all else was "vanity and a chasing after the wind" (Eccles. 6:9).

A self-emptying proclamation, a Jesus-based proclamation, cannot sound anything like that. What I didn't quite get then, but what subsequent life experience has made painfully clear, is that being a disciple of Jesus doesn't rid one of sin and imperfection. I know and stake my life on God's grace, but this doesn't give me a special place on the top of the hierarchy.

Christians are continually tempted to presuppose upon their special status in the world, claiming for themselves a holiness that makes them different from others; *and we are often unaware when we are doing this.* It is the opposite of self-emptying to proclaim that we have all truth and others have none of it, that our eternal fate is secure while all others are on their way to that Very Unpleasant Place—unless they listen to us in time.

Being followers of the One who emptied himself does not mean that we can't believe in salvation and eternal life. But it does deeply undercut the "us versus them" mentality, the sense that "we have it" and they don't. Proclamation that is oriented to Philippians 2 has one cardinal rule: I get to tell my story, but not in a way that places me above others. If I ever cease to be the servant of those around me in thought, word, and deed, then I have fallen away from Jesus' example. At that moment I've put myself on the top and them on the bottom, giving myself the pride of possession at their expense. Remember: the master is not greater than his disciple.

You can already begin to imagine the implications of this requirement. Talking about one's faith (proclamation) now becomes a form of dialogue, of giving *and* receiving. Of course, we don't have to believe that "everything is relative" and that we really have nothing to say. We do have deep convictions and a narrative to tell. As we've seen, ours is an unapologetically theological narrative, albeit one that's deeply personal at the same time. But along with the telling, we have a lot of listening to do—deep listening. We just can't be certain that all our interpretations of who Jesus was and what he revealed are flawless and inerrant, utterly without misunderstanding or prejudice on our part. Similarly, we can't know exactly what form discipleship will take in the ones with whom we are speaking. The Western church has learned an immense amount from Christian disciples in the churches in Africa, in Latin America (think of liberation theology!), in Asia, among indigenous peoples, in secularized Europe, among young people, and elsewhere. There are things to learn from outside the Christian world as well. The moment we stop being listeners, we have forgotten the lesson of self-emptying.

The criterion for staying on this path is not difficult. We only need to ask whether, in a given conversation, we are doing more learning and listening than teaching. If I'm not listening with my whole heart, how can I be open to the subtle promptings of the Spirit? From this first criterion another follows: if I stop liking the person I'm speaking to—if I don't feel as though this is a person with whom I'm ready to enter into real friendship—then I am probably not "speaking the truth in love." Indeed, perhaps I should not be speaking at all with this person at this time.

The same goes for ideas. As I blog and respond to others' blogs, and as I speak to audiences in the U.S. and abroad, I am continually confronted with new ideas. Those who think they have their "book talk" down, so that they can give it "with their eyes closed" to vastly different audiences in vastly different contexts, are deluding themselves. They have stopped listening. I do believe that God is related to absolutely everything that we encounter in this world, and I believe that Christ is relevant to all of it. But these various things and ideas connect to God and Christ in vastly different ways. It would be a complete illusion to claim that I understand all of these diverse relationships. One would need to know *a lot* about nuclear physics, evolutionary biology, the sociology of knowledge, ancient China, literary theory, the history of communism, and innumerable other things in order to determine in what incredibly complicated ways all these things are related to God's cosmic purposes.

One thing I know in advance: the answers will not be simple. Think about it: Christians have more reason within their very belief system to be life-long learners than anyone else: secularist, materialist, reductionist, or humanist. It doesn't take much meditation on the infinity of God to produce a rather large dose of humility in anyone who attempts to speak for God. When I meet people who are sure that they understand the relationship between God and world so fully that they can demonstrate that contemporary American customs (or the current practices of their church) are God's intended design for humanity, I can only shake my head in amazement. How could one know God's will so infallibly and not swell up with pride? The Jesus calling is to be a servant in the world of ideas—Christian servants, admittedly, but servants nonetheless.

Self-Emptying Theologies

I've keenly felt the dilemma raised by these last pages. Self-emptying is not the sole Christian message, nor is it a message that all Christians need to hear. Yet it was crucial that I model the start of an answer to the Seven Core Christian Questions that draws from Scripture, tradition, reason, and experience—and one that is personal and honest at the same time. The goal is not that you will leave the theological labors to me (or to anyone else), merely internalizing the results of someone else's work. The hope instead is that you will read these last pages so deeply that you'll be able to begin identifying your own theology, letting it emerge out of your own situation and then drawing from it the insights you need in order to grow into deeper discipleship in your own personal and communal context.

Still, your theology is not *reduced* to your situation and context. For Christians there must always be something authoritative in Christ's self-emptying. Moreover, the vast majority of us in Europe and North America enjoy positions of unimaginable power, comfort, and luxury compared to the Two-Thirds world. It doesn't take much travel in the Third World to realize that, if Jesus' sentence "they have received their reward" (Matt. 6:16) is true of anyone in the world today, it must be true of us. I thus suspect that the call to emulate the One who "humbled himself" may be particularly relevant to the theologies, and to the discipleship, of a large number of us.

There's one last reason for stressing this particular example. It has to do with the turn to postmodern believing that we explored earlier. For many men and women today, the claims to certainty made by "modern" Christians come across as the very opposite of self-emptying. Whatever the *intent* of those who proclaim that they have the full truth, or the perfect interpretation of Scripture, or the only path for the church to follow in today's world, the results are painful. To the ears of many of us in this postmodern world, a Christianity shorn of the condemnation of all other groups and individuals better conveys the spirit and message of the One whom we follow. As radical as it sounds, I suggest that we need to apply the attitude of self-emptying *even to our own Christian theologies.*

This new postmodern spirit—the quest to find common ground with others, even as we voice the distinctive features of our own faith—also promises to make us much more effective as we turn our attention from the needs of the church to the needs of our surrounding society. That, at any rate, is the argument I will be making in the few chapters that remain.

Part Three

Theologies That Can Transform Society

14. New Partnerships in Christian Activism

reat, so you have a new vision for Christian theology. You are learning to blend your life story with the narrative of God in Christ. You can begin to connect the Seven Core Christian Questions with significant events in your life. And, together with others, you're ready to sketch a theological vision that has the potential to transform the church. That's a powerful start!

By taking these steps, you join a vibrant group of believers who are seeking to think and live the relevance of Jesus' life and teaching for today's complex world. But how do Christian believers avoid freezing the results of this exciting work into a set of permanent dogmas? How do we keep the living ecosystem of a relationship with God's Spirit from turning into a petrified forest? Most urgently, how can we use our new theological visions as the basis for powerful action in society? After all, no matter how significant Christian fellowship may now become, our work's not done until we're having a transformative effect on the society around us as well.

The Obama Effect

Studies of American religious life are showing a new tendency, most prominent among young Americans, that gives ground for optimism. A recent article in *USA Today* dubbed it *pragmatic idealism*: "Meet the generation in which idealism trumps ideology, in which pragmatism is the guiding light."[1] Others are calling it "the Obama Effect."

Going back to the Pilgrims, the early settlers, and the pioneers, Americans have always tended to be a "can do" people. Since de Tocqueville's nineteenth-century classic, *Democracy in America*, Europeans have often commented on the "just do it!" attitude in this country. When the English would analyze, the Germans plan, and the French comment, Americans would roll up their sleeves and get the job done. You might think of the Amish ritual of "barn-raising" as an analogy for this American get-it-done mentality. In traditional Amish society, the extended family would work for weeks or months to prepare all the parts needed to put up a new building. On the designated day, friends and relatives and community members would be invited over to help assemble all the pieces. In traditional Amish society, the roles were assigned along strict gender lines; today we'd blend the roles a bit more. Together, the men put their shoulders under the pre-assembled walls and pivoted them up into place, holding them steady while others hammered in the nails. Women brought food and kept things running smoothly. Children helped as they could and otherwise played around the edges. By the end of the day the community, working as a team, was able to complete the basic structure, so that the rest of the work could be done by the family over the following weeks.

We see something of that same barn-raising spirit in the pragmatic idealism that commentators are detecting in American culture today. We saw it reflected in the Obama campaign, for example, and then in the style of presidency that it produced. A lot of us would watch the short videos and then click on the button to donate $10 or $20. Perhaps for the first time, we felt like we were participating in a political movement bigger than ourselves, something that would really make a difference.

Stephen Mansfield, author of *The Faith of Barack Obama* (Thomas Nelson, 2008), wrote recently in *USA Today* about President Obama's "big-tent approach" to religion and politics:

> This is what we can expect [from] a big tent faith-based presidency, rooted in a non-traditional approach to Christianity yet seeking to draw in nearly every religious tradition. For this, [Obama] understands, is how the majority of the people he serves would want it to be.[2]

Despite the harsh climate of recession (or perhaps even because of it?) this new phase in our history is bringing a resurgence of that traditional American optimism, that willingness to join with others in rolling up our sleeves and making things better. The Obama Phenomenon is both a symptom and a cause.

Postmodern (Pragmatic) Idealism

Now add to pragmatic idealism and President Obama's "big-tent approach" the postmodern mentality that we considered earlier. For many, especially younger Christians, the old boundaries and battle lines no longer divide as they once did. Of course discipleship will take many different forms and people will believe many different things. Of course it's a pluralistic world. There's nothing strange about alliances with a wide variety of people and groups. Sure it matters what people believe, but we don't want to be ideologues about it. What people actually do—as individuals, as congregations, and as participants in broader social movements—matters too. We're no longer willing to close off people whose beliefs are different from our own.

> *The old boundaries and battle lines no longer divide as they once did.*

Put all this together, and you have the makings of a "big tent" approach to Christian involvement in society of the sort we haven't seen for decades. That "big tent" spirit (Spirit) originally brought people together, literally under a single tent, during the Great Awakening. It reappeared when the original social gospel movement (Walter Rauschenbusch) swept across America. It was visible which *The Courage to Be* (Paul Tillich) was an American bestseller in the 1950s. It shined when the theologian Reinhold Niebuhr was writing books such as *Moral Man and Immoral Society* and consulting with American presidents. Christian activism to change society re-appeared in the early civil rights movement in the 1960s, the anti-war efforts during the Vietnam era, and the early feminist movement. And I suggest we're seeing it again as Christians begin to speak out strongly to reverse global warming and to preserve our natural environment on this planet.

In the postmodern context, Christian activism doesn't require a single account of faith shared by all participants. Everyone must have a reason to put his or her shoulder to the common work, of course. And it's important for all of us to consciously think through our reasons so that we are able to state them convincingly and powerfully. But no one single account has to win at the expense of the others, even among Christians.

15. Time to Leave behind Old Liberal/Evangelical Battles

We have chronicled the shift from modern to postmodern ways of thinking. We have seen what it means to practice Christian discipleship using the "Belonging, Behaving, Believing" method, and we've contrasted this method with the exclusionary way of thinking that typified the modern world. What do these shifts do to the old oppositions and battle lines that have defined the American church until recently?

It Looks Like "Liberal" Won't Do It

Webster's New World Dictionary defines *conservative* as "tending to preserve established traditions or institutions and to resist or oppose any changes in these [*conservative* politics, *conservative* art]." If the word *liberal* were just the antonym of *conservative*, it should therefore mean, "working to update, revise, or reform established traditions or institutions and to be open to changing them." Wouldn't that be a positive, even noble task to take on? But in fact the term *liberal* has suffered such a battering that it looks like it's down for the count. In many Christian circles, a liberal has come to mean something like the following:

- one who barely believes in God, if at all; someone who engages in a sort of narrow Nature worship—perhaps an outright pagan;
- one who ascribes no authority to the Bible or pokes holes in it; one who believes that the Bible contains a few morally helpful stories but who also notes that the same can be said of numerous novels, political manifestos, and non-Christian texts and traditions;

- one who views Jesus as (at best) a good ethical teacher and moral example, and at worst a misguided Galilean; one who rejects any special status for Jesus whatsoever;
- someone who does not want to talk about the resurrection or, if the subject comes up, tries to show that the whole story is an illusion—presumably just a statement about the subjective experiences of believers in subsequent centuries;
- one who holds the Christian tradition in complete disdain and seeks to deconstruct it in every way possible, gleefully destroying all inherited forms of Christian belief and ridiculing Christian practice;
- one who has no interest at all in the church, Christian worship, or personal discipleship; one who probably prefers other religious traditions to his or her own tradition (perhaps a crypto-Buddhist);
- one who cares more about community organizing than communion, about Bible-bashing than baptism, about inter-faith than personal faith, about vibrant politics more than a vibrant church;
- someone without hope in God's redemptive action or future work in the world, but actually a closet humanist who rests his or her faith on human potential alone; one who seeks to replace theology with science or with technological breakthroughs—in short, one who uses Christian language as merely a thin veneer for the "real" concerns, which are limited to matters of race, gender, class, overcoming oppression, and politics.

According to these stereotypes, "bleeding heart liberals" are people who hold superficial beliefs even about the things that matter most to them. Because they are so dogmatic about their liberal beliefs and so intolerant of all others, one just can't reason with them; it's best to steer clear of them.

It's interesting to read through this list of widely held beliefs about "liberals." I've never met such individuals, and, in fact, I doubt that they really exist. After all, that's how stereotyping works. One takes individual features that one doesn't like, or excesses of which given individuals have been guilty, or tendencies that are endemic to a movement. Out of them one creates a caricature, which is then put forward as the description of an entire group. Is it any wonder that Christian leaders across the country have cautioned me not to use the word *liberal* anywhere in this call for a renewal of Christian theology?

The process is just as invidious, by the way, when the targets are "conservatives" or "evangelicals." Tearing to shreds *any* member of the church in this manner is a destructive practice; it's usually inaccurate as well. An individual speaker may be trying to make some valid critical points (though I think speakers more often use these stereotypes in destructive ways). But people who are less subtle thinkers and those who tend to be unstable will take this vilification of individuals and groups to places that are extremely damaging, if not outright evil.

Consider one recent dramatic example: in May 2009 Scott Roeder walked into Reformation Lutheran Church in Wichita, Kansas, and shot Dr. George Tiller in cold blood while he was serving as an usher for the worship service. Dr. Tiller worked at a medical center and performed late-term abortions. Mr. Roeder, a long-time abortion foe with the e-mail name "ServantofMessiah," believed that murdering Dr. Tiller was an act of obedience to Jesus Christ. He was encouraged in this belief by some of the leaders in the Christian anti-abortion movement.[1] To the extent that these individuals encouraged violence, even murder, as a valid expression of their theological convictions, they share moral responsibility for the tragedy that occurred. It's a painful reminder of the consequences that can follow when leaders induce hatred and describe other persons as evil.

 Finding a Term that Splits the Difference

There are no signs of emerging neutral ground between liberals and the most conservative wings of the church. In fact, the negative connotations of the term *liberal* are so great that I doubt it can be used profitably within a "big tent" Christianity today. And yet we must have *some* positive term to describe what transforming theologies (in all their various forms) share in common. If we only use negative terms—*not* extreme right wing, *not* biblicist, *not* dogmatic or ideological—then we're engaging in exactly the same sort of negative campaigning that I've just been criticizing. It's not enough to keep repeating "not this; not this; not that. . . ."

Webster's New World defines *progressive* as "moving forward or onward . . . ; favoring, working for, or characterized by progress or improvement." One can work for progress without being committed to the whole range of doctrines known as *liberalism*. New Testament professor Hal Taussig offers a beautiful summary of progressive Christianity:[2]

- A spiritual vitality and expressiveness, including participatory, arts-infused, and lively worship as well as a variety of spiritual rituals and practices such as meditation;
- Intellectual integrity, including a willingness to question;
- An affirmation of human diversity;
- An affirmation of the Christian faith with a simultaneous sincere respect for other faiths;
- Strong ecological concerns and commitments;
- Social justice commitments.

Progressive does not exclude *evangelical*. Millions of Americans now describe themselves as "progressive evangelicals," following the lead of Jim Wallis and the Sojourners community. As an evangelical friend commented to me, "How can you be a Christian and *not* care about issues like peace, poverty, injustice, and the environment?"

Progressive does not represent an ideology but an emphasis. Consider the contrasts between this term and *conservative*. What does each express about the church's stance toward the modern world and thus about its role in contemporary society? Those who call themselves conservative want to focus more on "conserving" or retaining what Christians have received from the past. They do this because they believe that most beliefs and practices in contemporary secular society are opposed to the Christian tradition. They want the church to return to the practices and lifestyle of past decades or centuries. In short, they stress the *differences* between Christianity and contemporary society, between Christianity and other religions, and between what the church was in its golden age and what it is now.

By contrast, if you are a progressive, you will tend to emphasize change and newness in what the church is becoming. You don't have to hold to the modern doctrine called *meliorism*, the belief that the world is just getting better and better. But you do think there are

> *Progressive theologies emphasize change and newness in what the church is becoming.*

some positive things that we can learn from the contemporary world—from science, philosophy, technology, social movements, other religions, and so on. This doesn't mean that you disvalue the Christian tradition and seek to replace it with something different. But it does imply that you look for and value partnerships between contemporary culture and Christian faith, between the church and other organizations, between the past and the future. Again, being progressive does not mean that you wish to *reject* the past. But it does suggest a greater emphasis on innovation, on openness to change, on learning new things from new contexts, and on finding new forms through which the church and her action in the world may be manifested.

On the one hand, theology and politics are not identical. Being conservative theologically doesn't mean you have to be a political conservative, and being progressive theologically doesn't mean you have to affirm liberalism as your political philosophy. For instance, "progressive evangelicals" tend to be more conservative in their theologies and attitudes toward Scripture, while being more progressive in their politics. On the other hand, it's an illusion to think that the theological and the political dimensions are completely unrelated. People who are very conservative about their religion tend to be political conservatives as well. (Studies show they also tend to be conservative in their personalities.)

Since we must have a positive term—and knowing that there is no term that is free of all baggage—I will use the term *progressive* to describe constructive theologies that attempt to transform society. I know this decision is not without risk. As a leader of one of the major denominations said at the second Transforming Theology conference, "Many members of my communion would be deeply uncomfortable if they thought the head of their denomination had come to this conference to advocate progressive Christianity." Reading between the lines a bit, I assume the reason is that people would assume he was therefore an advocate of ordaining openly gay pastors, an issue over which his denomination is now deeply divided. *But it is not helpful to use "progressive" as a code word for* one *specific position over which Christians today are deeply divided.* In this book, "progressive" is not used to try to smuggle in a single answer to the debate about homosexuality. It would be disastrous to limit the use of the term in this way.

Progressive theologies represent a general approach to transforming society. A broad spectrum of theologies can therefore count as progressive. There are evangelical leaders who are clearly progressive in this broad sense but who affirm a more traditional or conservative answer on the question of ordaining actively gay clergy. There are progressives at the other end of the spectrum who strongly advocate liberal political positions on most or all of the contentious issues in the church and in our society today. Organizations such as Progressive Christians Uniting and the Network of Spiritual Progressives, for example, stand toward the left end of this spectrum. Folks in the mainline denominations locate themselves at virtually every point along the continuum.

Whatever happens, don't let battles about terms bring your striving for a "big tent," transformative Christianity to a standstill. Wars over words are tragic and wasteful. Followers of Jesus can't afford them, for we have urgent and important work to get done. When you despair of overcoming the divisions within the church today, look to examples of people you admire who are really making a difference. Read and learn from authors who don't fall into particular camps but who bridge over differences. I think, for example, of Glen Stassen, one of the Transforming Theology participants. Glen teaches at Fuller, an evangelical seminary. At the same time, he has been at the forefront of the "just peacemaking" movement.[3] Glen writes extensively about the burning social and political issues of our day, but also about the biblical foundations of just peacemaking. And he uses the Seven Core Christian Questions as a way to build bridges from the biblical texts to the contexts of our day. If anyone tells you that you have to choose between biblical and theological sources on the one hand, and powerful, prophetic activism in today's world on the other, tell them to work through one of Glen Stassen's works.

Making a Difference with the Difference

Transforming Theology is not about advocating one particular theological position. It is not a manifesto; it is a movement—or, more accurately, a network of networks. Thus you'll find within the movement not "the" theological answer but a wide range of theological proposals, just as they're arising today in the context of transformative Christian life in church and society. Only if we consciously welcome many diverse voices does it make sense to speak of the one "big tent" of reflective Christian voices in our society today.

Thus we prefer to understand progressive theology as a *style or mode* of Christian believing and acting. Think of it as a call to Christian activism that keeps one eye on the distinctive features of Jesus' life and ministry, the other eye on the world that's unfolding around us. We have to learn from and about *both* if we're to bring them into redemptive relationship. That means that we can't just focus on a set of abstract Christian doctrines on the one hand, or on techniques for church growth or community organizing on the other.

Progressive Christians emphasize that theologies are always developed and lived out in the context of Christian life, worship, and ministry. Thus we emphatically break with the centuries-old stereotype, according to which theologians in monasteries, universities, and seminaries decide what the right theology is, so that active clergy and laypersons can then put it into practice. *Theologies are the products of Christians in ministry in society* and express their needs and insights.

This changes everything. When people in transforming churches and transforming ministries describe the beliefs that motivate their ministries, what do they say? When they sometimes pause, as they must, to say how their experience in the world influences their answers to the Seven Core Christian Questions, what new emphases and insights do they bring? I presuppose that theologies are composed in the trenches, not in ivory towers. For this reason I invite ordinary people into the dialogue, not just the specialists. I invite you to become *producers* of Christian theologies and not merely *consumers* of theologies.

This is why I resist the tendency to insist that there is *a* correct progressive theology that should serve as the norm and authority for all genuine Christian action in church and society. Instead, as we'll see in a moment, progressive theologies reveal important family resemblances. They emphasize similar priorities that we can discern across a wide range of Christian responses to the social challenges of our day.

In fact, doesn't this *have to be* the response of any approach to theology that is progressive? Conservatives might be tempted to formulate a precise version of "the truth once given"—as a few leaders did when they wrote and publicized the "Evangelical Manifesto" of 2008. But progressive Christians insist that we must be continually responding to the world as it is changing and developing. This requires formulating new and ever deeper understandings of Jesus' life and of the biblical teachings, in continual dialogue with actual ministries in churches and in society. It's in that spirit that we turn to the next major section of this project.

16. From Church Ministries to Missional Churches

W e've made a good start. Subdividing the church into the opposing camps of liberals and conservatives and then allowing them to engage in a fight to the death was a recipe for disaster. However, the rethinking has to go much, much deeper. It turns out that the whole idea of separating "the life of the church" from its "external" ministry programs—which was the dominant pattern in the modern period—is neither biblical nor effective. As churches have slid more and more to the margins of our society, this strategy has proven increasingly damaging. Truly transformational theologies, and the activism that accompanies them, will have to set out from a completely different set of assumptions about church and society.

 ## How Things Used to Be

The new paradigm is so different from the assumptions of the modern approach to missions that it's difficult to find common language to talk about the two together. What's happening today is definitely not the same as the "calls to mission" that we would hear as students at my conservative evangelical college several decades ago. The speaker would generally describe some area of the world—hopefully as exotic sounding as possible—where most people were not Christians. He would tell us that God's work was to win these people for Christ. We and the speaker knew that there were multiple "means" for winning people for Christ. They had names like "friendship evangelism" or "tent-making ministries." One might begin with acts of charity or with social justice ministries. But eventually one would be able to tell the people why he was doing all these good things or why the love that he and his fellow Christians showed was so distinctive. At that point he would "proclaim Christ," which we all hoped would lead to the conversion of his non-Christian listeners.

The new approaches to mission are also not like the "social justice ministries" that played such a major role in the mainline churches during the twentieth century. Although the popular conception of liberal churches is that liberals never depend on the Bible, in fact social justice ministries *often* began with Scripture verses such as Matthew 25 (to which we return below) and with theological concepts such as the kingdom of God, the special call to minister to the poor and downtrodden, and Jesus' own examples of ministry. The social justice model usually begins with one's home base in the church, where preaching, fellowship, and teaching make members aware of the "preferential option" for the poor and needy. Church-based ministries then identify where the downtrodden and outcast are in the community or society; a church or para-church ministry is planned to reach out to these people; and much of the financial support comes from the church communities. Those working for social justice return regularly to their home church community, often exhausted and discouraged. There the preaching of the coming kingdom of God and the eschatological hope buoy them up again so that they can return to the work. The immediate goal of social justice ministries is not to convert people to Christ and to pray the Sinner's Prayer with them. But I think it's generally assumed that at least some of the people affected by social justice ministries will eventually start attending a local church.

Now both of these traditional forms of ministry may have their drawbacks and abuses. *But neither of them is inherently bad.* It's just that there are some radically new ways of conceiving ministry afoot today, which are closely connected to the "postmodern believing" that we discussed earlier. This chapter is about this new understanding of ministry. Rather than inventing a new term to confuse people, I follow standard practice and speak of them as *missional* approaches.

How Things Are Now

Tom Sine is the author of the immensely popular book, *The Mustard Seed Conspiracy* (W Pub Group, 1981). In 2008 he published a sequel, *The New Conspirators* (InterVarsity), in which he offers instructions for "creating the future one mustard seed at a time." In Conversation One he urges churches to become "emerging, missional, mosaic, and monastic." This means developing much deeper connections between the everyday practices of "church life" and a missional, outward-directed orientation. The emerging churches, he finds, are already beginning to make these connections. He writes:

- Emerging leaders are much more into gospel as story, narrative and metaphor and have little interest in a propositional, dogmatic approach to theology common in many conservative churches.
- Emerging churches, informed by their postmodern instincts, tend to be highly experimental and artistic, often working compellingly with both image and word . . . [they] tend to offer multilayered, experiential worship that draws on both ancient symbols and images from "profane" culture.
- Emerging leaders are committed to calling people to a more authentic, embodied, whole-life faith.
- Emerging churches, by their very nature, tend to be outwardly focused in mission, not only to engage a specific group, but with a desire to have an impact on the lives of people in their communities and the larger world.
- Emerging churches are relational, organic and communal with virtually no bureaucratic hierarchical modes of leadership, unlike many denominational and non-denominational churches.
- Emerging churches tend to be concerned about a broad range of social issues, including social justice, reconciliation and creation care.[1]

Once again, Tom Sine is onto something important. What are the assumptions that led people to separate "internal" church life from "external" ministries in the first place? And what does it look like when we replace the modern approach with a new set of postmodern assumptions?

Rethinking the Theology of Mission from the Ground Up

The modern idea of "missions" was developed at a time when the Christian church thought of itself as the only religious game in town. In fact, American life was never exclusively Christian. We were always a culture of Christians *and* Jews—along with Native Americans, dozens of other religions from around the world, and many atheists and otherwise non-religious persons. Still, as long as Christians perceived American culture as a "Christian culture," missions tended to mean *overseas* missions. We traveled elsewhere to win heathen peoples for Christ. For decades, as you probably know, mainline churches and denominations have been giving decreasing amounts of support to missions in this sense. *But the mindset hasn't yet changed.* Missions still tends to mean what other people do "over there."

The "only game in town" mentality also assumes that, if Christians don't do the kind of charitable work that religious people do, no one else will. So church people would leave the safety of their four walls to engage in ministries of care for the poor, peacemaking, social justice, community organizing, and so forth. The trouble is, the underlying assumption was false. As Diana Eck shows in her immensely influential book, *A New Religious America* (HarperOne, 2001), the United States today is the most religiously diverse nation in the world.

This changes everything. "We need to recognize," writes Dan Kimball, "that America is a nation that offers an ever more accessible mix of spiritual choices, all perceived as equal."[2] This new reality doesn't just affect evangelism and mission in the traditional sense; *it affects everything we do outside of church buildings.* (In fact, as I'll show, it should affect much of what we do *inside* those buildings as well!) In a marginal note printed in the same book, Brian McLaren puts the point forcefully:

> If we don't realize that we are [already] missionaries in a foreign culture (and that, in fact, every culture is a foreign culture), we'll just resort to saying our spiel more and saying it louder. This has been our strategy in the U.S. during my lifetime, I think. Get "Jesus" on as many billboards, bumper stickers, TV shows, and sports broadcasts as possible, and God will do the rest. If they're not listening, shout louder, sweat harder, and get angrier. The result, sadly, is that we make "Jesus" seem like a cheap slogan. We could just as well be shouting, "Enron! Enron!" or "Plastics! Plastics!" and we make ourselves look like kooks who don't know the difference between speaking and communicating. Someone should ask us, "Why did Jesus speak in parables?"[3]

Missional thinking is thinking after Christendom, after "the Christian nation," after "cultural Christianity." It's talking about Jesus' Way when the gospel is no longer taken as a matter of course, when being an American and being "a church member in good standing" are no longer seen as synonymous.

It's answering the Seven Core Christian Questions without assuming that others already care about the questions. More radically, it involves restructuring the life of Christian communities on the assumption that these changes pertain not only outside churches *but inside them as well.*

Features of Missional Churches

The quickest way to communicate what missional approaches involve is to read the stories of those who practice them. What are they doing, and what kinds of theologies are they developing out of their actions? For five years Eddie Gibbs and Ryan Bolger conducted in-depth interviews and discussions with dozens of such leaders. *Emerging Churches: Creating Christian Community in Postmodern Cultures* summarizes the discoveries from their years of research. Here are their central results:

> Emerging churches are not young adult services, Gen-X churches, churches-within-a-church, seeker churches, purpose-driven or new paradigm churches, fundamentalist churches, or even evangelical churches. They are a new expression of church. The three core practices are *identifying with the life of Jesus, transforming secular space,* and *commitment to community as a way of life.* These practices are expressed in or lead to the other six: *welcoming the stranger, serving with generosity, participating as producers, creating as created beings, leading as a body,* and *taking part in spiritual activities.*[4]

The detailed examples of these nine core practices are worth close study. But what I find even more fascinating are the nearly 100 pages of personal stories of emergent leaders, told in their own words. The words of Dieter Zander, the founder of Quest in Novato, California, will give you a taste. Dieter describes his work with neighborhood-based faith communities:

> We gather to do good news to the neighborhood. The groups meet to be servant-oriented to the neighborhood. We meet, first, to be with other Christians and, second, to reimagine life with God, rethink the gospel, and reapply it as a practical outworking of doing good in the world in Jesus' name. Each of us seeks to be a coworker with Jesus, flowing from the gospel.[5]

Eddie Gibbs and Ryan Bolger do not mince words. The West, they argue, is in the midst of "huge cultural shifts," and the church has not kept up. "Much of what we understand as historical church practices is simply cultural adaptations that occurred at other times and places in church history. The church must 'de-absolutize' many of its sacred cows in order to communicate afresh the good news to a new world."[6] They cite Karen Ward (of Church of the Apostles in Seattle) who notes, "Ninety-five percent of the non-churched have a favorable view of Jesus, so Jesus is not the problem." The authors then comment, "In a time of immense cultural change and disconnect with the church, emerging churches retrieved the Jesus of the Gospels but not necessarily the Christ of history."[7]

> *Understand the postmodern world, engage it, and get ready for revolution!*

About ten years ago Brian McLaren published *The Church on the Other Side: Doing Ministry in the Postmodern Matrix*. The basic message of his proposal was unmistakable: "Enter the postmodern world," which means: "Understand it . . . engage it . . . and get ready for revolution."[8] Yet many of his ideas are still being disregarded. I summarize them here as a starting point. You don't have to implement the ideas in the exact ways that Brian suggests. But if these ideas still seem revolutionary to you, you and your church colleagues probably need to wrestle more deeply with the new context in which the church exists today:

1. *Maximize discontinuity*: distinguish between renewed, restored, and reinvented churches, and focus on the last;
2. *Redefine your mission*: clarify and simplify to "more Christians, better Christians" in authentic missional community, for the good of the world;
3. *Practice systems thinking*: see the church program in terms of inter-related systems rather than quick fixes;
4. *Trade up your traditions for tradition*: distinguish between church traditions and *the* Christian Tradition, and move emphasis from the former to the latter;
5. *Resurrect theology as art and science*: stop thinking of theology as a matter of technical training, in which answers are already known, and rejuvenate theology through a quest for truth and beauty;

6. *Design a new apologetic*: find fresh ways to communicate the gospel to the postmodern mind;

7. *Learn a new rhetoric*: realize that old communication patterns are less and less effective in the new world, and discover new, appropriate modes of discourse;

8. *Abandon structures as they are outgrown*: adopt a new paradigm for church structure that allows for routine reengineering based on changes in size, constituency, resources, and strategy.[9]

We're talking about new ways of thinking about ministry in a postmodern world—ways so different from old ways of thinking that many of us don't even call them "ministries" any more. The new ways speak powerfully to members of a new generation that is no longer moved by the old language and techniques in the way that earlier generations were. If you want to know who these people are, just look around to see who is *not* getting teary-eyed when the congregation sings "How Great Thou Art" or "In the Garden."

17. Social Transformation without "Us versus Them"

C hristians still want to make a difference in the world. It's our calling, and our passion. Yet now it's a different world than the one for which most of our established ministries were designed. How are we going to transform it if we don't understand it? In this new world:

- Meeting on Sunday mornings with a local church congregation in a church building may no longer be the home base, social center, and launching pad for what one does in the world.
- Unlike modern approaches to ministry, one can no longer separate sharply between church life, worship, mission, and ministry. Worship, Bible study, and Christian fellowship are already missional. What once was external ministry—meeting with people outside the church as *they* struggled to understand who Jesus was and how he might be significant for their lives—is now a part of the religious identity of many people *within* the church.
- New technologies are creating new forms of Christian community that the world has never known before. *No one understands how the new forms of social networking and communication will transform what it means to be church even ten or twenty years from now.*
- Through all these changes, the lines between "inside" and "outside" have become increasingly blurred. As a result, people today have trouble beginning with the conviction that "we have it" and "they lack it."

If you read that last sentence with "modern" eyes, you probably inferred that these people are relativists who don't really care about Jesus. They have sold

Christianity down the river; they no longer believe the message of salvation; and they have no message of hope to offer a starving world. You're free to have your own opinion, but please at least notice that that's not how missional Christians see it. Identities *really are* more complex in today's world.

Our Plural Identities

In an earlier chapter I argued that the new order is "Belong, Behave, Believe," not "Believe, Behave, Belong." One of the reasons is that each of us—Christian, Jew, Muslim; American, Chinese, Kenyan—belongs more places than we can count. You may be a cradle Christian who encountered Buddhism and existentialism in college and social justice ministries after that. I was raised atheist and had a dramatic conversion to Christ in high school. You may have as a friend a former evangelical who says she can no longer believe, yet she may be fully as preoccupied with Christian claims as you are. With such complex, interwoven identities, is it any surprise that authentic discipleship takes different forms in different contexts?

I'm guessing that most readers already know the experience of living in a deeply pluralistic world. If you're one of those people, an interwoven identity is second-nature to you; it's the air you breathe. *Of course* Christian identities are not rigid and fully definable in "essentialist" fashion, you say. All important identities weave their roots in, around, and through everything that we are. Our family, our language, our culture, the color of our skin—how could we separate our life of faith from these things?

In this new world we have to listen really hard to understand another's identity. Judging others has become way more complex. Have we then merely become relativists, folks who can no longer be disciples with our entire heart, soul, strength, and mind? By no means! If there was time, we could walk through the major moments in Jesus' ministry when he showed incredible awareness of the complexity of human identities, for example in John 4, Luke 7, and Luke 10. No one would call Jesus a relativist.

Like you, I wish the world were as clear, as black and white, as it once was. Identities in this new world, like families, are often "blended." (Just ask people under the age of twenty-five how many families they know where there has always been a biological mom and dad and two kids all living together.) Consider, for example, how complex is the identity of an American teenager in L. A. whose parents were born in Mexico. She speaks accent-free English, but also Spanish; she attends a mixed-race school with more cultures and languages than she can count; her Catholic church blends Hispanic and Anglo traditions; she wants to go to Harvard but her parents want her to stay close to her extended family. Who is she really?

Well, our religious identities have become no less complex. "Inside" and "outside," "Christian" and "non-Christian," "church" and "non-church"— identities flow and mix together in ways we can scarcely reconstruct. The cradle Christian who no longer believes may still be culturally Christian and appear Christian to outsiders (as the nineteenth-century Danish theologian Søren Kierkegaard so powerfully described). By contrast, the new postmodern disciple who lives in an utterly secular world, with very little Christian socialization in his background or among his friends, may look to your eyes pretty "non-Christian"—even though his discipleship to Jesus and the living God is the most important thing in his life.

 ## Theology in an Age of Interlocking Identities

The next two decades will bring technological and social changes more rapid and revolutionary than anything this planet has ever experienced. Rigidifying the past won't help us learn to be church in new and powerful ways for this new context. But boldly finding new ways to be Jesus' arms and legs in the world will. What it means to do theology in and for this new age just won't be the same, though it will be equally important. It's going to take some serious thought on our part to figure it out.

The great thing about the world of conservative Christian missions in which I was trained was that theology was built into it right from the start. We knew the Scripture verses that supported world missions ("Go ye therefore, and teach all nations, baptizing them in the name of the Father, and of the Son, and of the Holy Ghost" Mt. 28:19-20 [KJV]). We knew how to embed those verses in theologies that included doctrines of God, Christ, Spirit, salvation, church, and the Second Coming. The only trouble was that the theologies we employed didn't do much listening to the world around us. We read about other religions in order to show why they were wrong and we were right, or in order to find "redemptive analogies" (as Alan Richardson put it in his 1975 work, *Peace Child*) that we could use in missions and evangelism. There were of course authors who made things more complex. I think in particular of Bishop Lesslie Newbigin, whose wisdom and depth had a major, even transformative impact on many of us as we began to think more deeply about mission, and I think of Stanley Skreslet's recent book on images of mission in the New Testament.[1]

It wasn't just missions work, though. Social justice ministries likewise were built, at least at the start, upon deep biblical and theological foundations. Just pick up Walter Rauschenbusch's classic 1907 work, *Christianity and the Social Crisis* (it's still in print!). Or read *Radical Monotheism and Western Culture* by H. Richard Niebuhr; the Niebuhrs' renewed theological call to social justice ministries in the mid-20th century had a profound impact on the church and American society. Most Latin American liberation theologies likewise had a strong biblical and theological base, although they also drew from Marxist sources. And I am always struck by how deeply the speeches of Dr. Martin Luther King Jr. drew from biblical theological sources and how close to the surface they remain. In fact, in the historically black churches the foundations in Bible and theology have *stayed* close to the surface over the last forty years. Here—in sermons, in books, and in the everyday language of church people—the worlds of theology and social justice interweave in a rich tapestry of belief, conviction, and action.

How is it, then, that folks in the mostly white mainline churches have lost touch with this heritage? We know that it's good to support social justice ministries, and we're sure that there must be deep Christian reasons for them. It's just that we seem to have forgotten what they are! Have we become shy about using distinctively Christian language, perhaps out of fear of seeming to exclude other religions? We value social justice work, and we frequently talk about this value. But if we can't ground it in our own Christian tradition and language, our own actions will eventually fail to make sense even in our own eyes.

A Call to Retrieval, Renewal—and Radical Transformation

It's time to retrieve and renew our own heritage. Let's go back and search the Scriptures to find that thing that we once knew and have now somehow forgotten. Let's read old passages with new eyes, trying to understand what are the Christian roots and reasons for ministries to the poor and oppressed. Even more radically, let's rediscover what "ministry" was in Jesus' life and in the early church. Let's be like Nehemiah, who presided over the rediscovery of the Law of Moses and a renewed study of the texts (Neh. 8:13). I suggest that *the new approaches we've been practicing in this book offer a good, and perhaps even an indispensable framework for rekindling theological imagination that can lead to transformative action.*

This is where the postmodern rethinking of mission is so crucial. The standard evangelical and liberal approaches to Christian ministry were both modern, albeit in their different ways. They were built up upon clear distinctions: in the one case, those who had Christ in contrast to those who needed Christ; in the other case, us helping the needy, or the oppressed resisting the powerful oppressors—or in general the good guys versus the bad guys.

> There are ways to rekindle theological imagination that leads to transformative action.

Missional discipleship to Jesus begins when all these categories become so complex and convoluted that they start to deconstruct. (For many of us, the old categories are like a knitted sweater that started to unravel, so that after awhile all we had was a tangle of yarn.) You know you want to be a disciple of Jesus. You believe, as I do, that his life and teaching, his death and resurrection, still have something to say to the incredibly complex issues that humanity has to address immediately if we (and most of the other species on this planet) are going to make it through the next few years. But applying Christian beliefs to such difficult problems is a really complex task. Many people long for the days when life was more like a cowboy movie, where the Good Guys and the Bad Guys were so clearly marked that *nobody* could doubt which was which. (I think George W. Bush saw the world this way.) But today's world is more like *The Gods Must Be Crazy* than like a classic western.

The starting point is the same one we discovered in Part 2: *we have to learn to tell our story, as individuals and as communities, together with Jesus' story.* If we can do that, we can begin to reinterpret classic Christian language for our own day; we can learn to speak in new Christian dialects, as it were, to today's challenges. Should we fail in this task, I fear that the old Christian concepts will forever remain a foreign language to most people.

Try it. (The "Conversations Worth Having" in part 4 offer a good starting point.) As soon as you begin, you learn three things. First, telling your own story can be difficult—identities really are complex in today's world.

Next, you realize that your story is not all about you. Your story may *start* as a personal narrative, an autobiography. But it's also the story of your family, your ethnicity, and your country of origin. As it expands outward, it also becomes the story of your age, the history of your religion, the narrative of your religion intersecting with other religions. For believers, it also becomes the story of God's self-revelation; and for Christians, our story is also the story of God's redemptive work in Christ.

The third thing you learn is that you can't tell your story without thinking about your most deeply held beliefs. Stories entail beliefs, though they may be sub- or unconscious. When Jack works overtime in order to make more money, rather than pursuing his hobbies or hanging out with his friends, he reflects the belief that wealth (or at least financial security) is especially important. Laticia's pursuit of power in her law firm, or Juanita's volunteer work and charitable contributions, or Hans and Ursula's decision to relocate to Minnesota's Twin Cities after retirement in order to be closer to their grandchildren—each of these life decisions expresses deeply held beliefs, beliefs that matter.

For followers of Jesus, at least some of these beliefs will be theological beliefs—beliefs about the Seven Core Christian Questions that we've been discussing throughout this book. You may have been taught from an early age that evangelism is central to the Christian life, or that social justice ministries are the essence of Christian witness. Or perhaps you're from a world where no one talked about any of these topics. It doesn't matter, for in any case the question is still the same: how can we state what we believe in such an effective and vibrant way that it will motivate powerful, transformative action in the world?

18. Constructing Theologies of the Community for the Community: The Six Steps

I n this chapter I offer six steps for developing Christian theologies that support social transformation. In the past, the standard way of describing the task has been to create *a theology for Christian involvement in broader society.* The trouble is that each of those words carries baggage; the connotations point in the wrong directions. "Involvement in society" sounds like an (external) obligation—sort of like having to do "community service" after you've been convicted of a crime. "Christian" in this context suggests something like a voting bloc. It certainly connotes "Us versus Them"—or at least an insider/outsider mentality that puts "us" on the other side of the fence from "them." And preceding the whole thing by "theology" makes it sound like there will be some cold system of requirements, abstract principles, and ethical mandates, all of which will be laid on the shoulders of innocent, well-meaning folks like the yoke of the cart is laid on the shoulders of tired oxen. We need to approach the whole question in a radically different way.

 The Excitement Principle

Notice how things change when one moves outward from the starting place we've identified in earlier chapters. Here are the first three steps:

1. Go back to the story you've learned to tell about what draws you to Jesus' Way and how Jesus' life and teachings are relevant to how you want to live.

2. Add the answers to the Seven Core Christian Questions that you have started to develop. Remember, it's not sufficient to give answers that you have memorized from other sources; you have

to list what you can actually affirm. (It's better to give minimal answers that are really your own than to list a bunch of propositions that someone else has told you that you have to affirm.)

3. Reflect on the kinds of actions that you can genuinely take part in, actions that stem from your experience (question 1) and your actual beliefs (question 2).

Why begin with these first three steps? Folks in mainline churches have had so many heavy ministry obligations laid on their shoulders that a sort of "compassion fatigue" has set in. Many church people feel so guilty about all the forms of oppression that exist and all the ways that they are complicit in the suffering of others that they walk around like zombies. They'd rather do anything than come to church for another serving of guilt. It reminds me of those days early in the environmental movement when we cluttered our kitchens with twenty-six different recycling receptacles and still felt guilty about what we were wasting. Increased political and environmental sensitivity *is* important, but creating guilt is not the way to get there. People will not begin to pour themselves with passion into social justice ministries as long as these ministries are hung around their necks like albatrosses and held in place with the heavy chains of guilt.

Contrast the guilt approach to social justice ministries with the way that "witnessing" is traditionally taught within evangelical churches. In the churches of my youth, "sharing your faith" was expected. But we didn't experience it as a chore or burden. Our spiritual lives were filled with excitement from encountering the risen Jesus, experiencing the grace of God and the power of the Holy Spirit, and believing that we had just been reborn. Witnessing simply meant sharing that excitement with the people we met.

We could fight about the relative importance of winning souls for Christ versus social ministries and community organizing. But that's not the point here. *The excitement principle—the personal involvement and conviction—can be the same in both cases!* Whether you agree with them or not, the reborn Christians I just described act out of a deep passion and conviction that is fully consistent with their particular theology. There's no reason that mainline Christians can't find a similar excitement, one that is equally consistent with their own theological commitments and personal narratives.

A brief example: an African American seminary student named Chrystal walked into my office today. She's in the middle of a full-time summer internship, working with a ministry that provides shelters for homeless people. It's really hard work; some of these are bruised and broken people, and they can be very demanding. But Chrystal is on fire about her work. She tells me with passion about her own evolving theology, a strong incarnational theology that places a strong emphasis on Matthew 25. Plus, she is learning a lot about herself, about different social classes, and about people and life in general. Excitement sparkles in her eyes as she describes what she's learning.

The moral is simple: the kingdom of God would be a lot better off if people went hunting for the kinds of conversations and actions that brought that sparkle of excitement to their eyes. Imagine a Sunday morning church service where even a third of the congregation had been involved, even briefly, in conversations and actions of this sort during the preceding week. (Maybe they don't even call them "ministries"!) Imagine the energy this would bring to their worship and prayer. And imagine the impact that this congregation would be having on its community.

Perhaps you've been a member of congregations that have rediscovered the passion of missional living. I've seen many successful examples:

- A Quaker meeting where members stood in silent witness between gay rights activists and anti-homosexual activists during a major protest. They felt fear, but also grace, and they were still talking about it months later.
- A Presbyterian church in which a large group was involved in building a water purification plant in Mexico. From the tech experts to the translators to the logistics people to the simple helpers—everyone was buzzing about this shared project of ministry. (They gave the phrase "toilet talk" a whole new meaning.)
- A youth group that had just returned from assisting the victims of Hurricane Katrina in New Orleans. These young men and women had a brand-new understanding of their Christian identity. Ask them about it ten years from now; it was a life-changing experience. (Imagine what would happen if we sent our young men and women to assist in inner-city schools rather than to fight wars overseas. The differences would last for a lifetime or longer.)

And the examples go on and on.

Identifying with a Missional Community

Now we can add the next three steps to the three we've already covered. Here's the entire list:

1. Describe what draws you to Jesus' Way and how his life and teachings are relevant to how you want to live.
2. Add the answers to the Seven Core Christian Questions that you have started to develop.
3. Reflect on the kinds of actions that you can genuinely take part in that stem from your experience and your actual beliefs.
4. Now consider the community or communities with which you identify. Answer question 3 again, but this time with "you" plural (the community) rather than just "you" singular.
5. List what you need to know in order to carry out the actions in question 4 most effectively. What do you need to know about the people with and for whom whom you'll be working? What do you need to know about their backgrounds, cultures, needs and wishes? About the surrounding environment, social networks, economic realities, and political situation?
6. Now construct your plan of action.

Here's the big challenge in carrying out these last three steps: we Americans have forgotten how to tell corporate stories. Identity in traditional societies is *primarily* communal and social. Just think of books such as *Things Fall Apart* by Chinua Achebe or *The Good Earth* by Pearl S. Buck. Think of how one's particular village or region plays a central role in one's story in traditional Europe, Africa, or Asia. Traditional American society also knew something of corporate stories—from the "manifest destiny" view that accompanied the westward expansion of Europeans across the American continent (not always a pretty story), to the stories of various immigrant peoples coming to the "promised land," to the regional identities that have played such a large role in the history of this country. (Are you from south or north of the Mason-Dixon line?)

But today most Americans no longer know how to tell corporate stories. Can you even name your great-grandparents, or your grandparents' siblings? How often do you get together for family reunions of a dozen people or more? Most of my kids' friends don't know the experience of an intact nuclear family, much less of any sort of extended family—and that's not even to mention broader communal identities. If it's really true that "it takes a village to raise a child," then our society is in deep trouble.

We also connect less at the national level than we once did. The events following 9/11 created a surge of patriotism, even though much of it was driven by fear or even hatred. Soldiers who have fought in Iraq or Afghanistan score higher on measures of patriotism, but one would hate to think that taking up arms is the only way to help people bond with their nation. True, the Obama campaign and the early months of his presidency have created a huge upsurge of patriotic spirit. "Yes, we can" (like the phrase Deval Patrick used while running for governor of Massachusetts, "together we can") expressed a sense of identification with a national political movement on a scale hardly seen in recent decades. Still, the Obama campaign may be the exception that proves the rule. Indeed, the decreased involvement of voters in the legislative battles that have broken out *since* the election of 2008 suggests that Americans are again returning to our individualistic ways.

The struggle of local church congregations to remain vital and growing communities has everything to do with this deep-rooted American tendency. Of course, we can use the language of "the body of Christ" and "not neglecting to meet together" (Heb. 10:25), but the evidence suggests we don't naturally think in such communal terms, at least not at the core of our everyday life. I venture to suggest that many people (at least in the sixteen to twenty-six age range, but probably outside it as well) put more of themselves into their comments on Facebook than they do into their social interactions on Sunday mornings. Some feel they are more "being themselves" when they answer that question at the top of their Facebook home page—"What's on your mind?"—than when they shake hands with acquaintances over a cup of coffee in Fellowship Hall after the service.

 ## Why Real Community and Missional Christianity are Inseparable

There was a time when participating in a Christian community met so many functions, religious and otherwise, that it stood right at the center of one's identity for many, if not most, Americans. Until recently, the remains of these functions still kept people closely tied to their congregations. However, for people under the age of fifty today, *very few of these motivations are still*

in place. Our entire social existence and structure has changed. To look for a socially transformative theology without addressing the new context is futile. We need to state the truth of the situation if we're to get to the bottom of things.

The truth is that over the last several decades, Christian community and Christian ministries have worked (when they did work) because the people involved liked being together. They liked being together because they felt that they had important things in common, that they were learning from each other, and that they were making a significant difference in the world. Today, a decreasing number of Americans under the age of fifty feel this way about attending a mainline church (if they still attend one) or being involved in corporate Christian ministries. *But the same people do experience those three qualities in some of the other communal activities they engage in.* Therefore we need to first understand what makes these new types of community successful. How are they different from the kinds of associations Americans engaged in forty or fifty years ago, the associations on which our present congregational structures are based? Where can we find emerging forms of Christian community engaged in new forms of social ministry?

The results are clear: in today's world, successful ministries—ministries with which people really identify—presuppose and grow out of a vibrant sense of community. Many of us know this from youth work. Successful youth groups create powerful communal bonds because the kids' experiences are similar in many ways. When you're successful, you often feel like you were only a minor catalyst for a bunch of bonding that was already there, pent up, just waiting to happen.

Mainline churches that are predominantly white are having the hardest time meeting this goal. In our society, being white and a member of a mainline church just isn't enough to create the needed sense of community. By contrast, in churches that are predominantly African American, Hispanic American, or Asian American, it's more usual for members to bond based on shared experiences, shared interests, and shared needs. Barack Obama writes with deep insight into why this is so:

> I was drawn to the power of the African American religious tradition to spur social change. Out of necessity, the black church *had* to minister to the whole person. Out of necessity, the black church rarely had the luxury of separating individuals from collective salvation. It had to serve as the center of the community's political, economic, and social as well

as spiritual life; it understood in an intimate way the biblical call to feed the hungry and clothe the naked and challenge powers and principalities. In the history of these struggles, I was able to see faith as more than just a comfort to the weary or a hedge against death; rather, it was an active, palpable agent in the world. In the day-to-day work of the men and women I met in church each day, in their ability to "make a way out of no way" and maintain hope and dignity in the direst of circumstances, I could see the Word made manifest.[1]

This bonding—this commitment to a full gospel, an embodied gospel—is the heart of transformative Christian presence in society.

But where do people go for religious community when they are in their late twenties and in extremely demanding professional jobs? Where do they go for religious fellowship when they are single and in their late thirties? Very large churches can sometimes host vibrant groups based on the shared needs and interests of these particular groups, and in turn they can nourish powerful forms of missional Christianity. Part of the tragedy of declining membership in the mainline is that most congregations are far too small to have the "critical mass" needed to support such groups.

> "The black church understood . . . the biblical call to feed the hungry and clothe the naked and challenge powers and principalities."
>
> Barack Obama,
> The Audacity of Hope

When ministries are successful, generally you'll find that real community has been formed. Watch the dynamics of a Christian startup being run by visionary young men and women, all of whom are living on a shoestring budget, are filled with idealism, and are working with a "let's get it done" attitude. Or watch a Korean American ministry, where shared values and a shared work ethic help things to function smoothly. Or watch a Christian ministry that is staffed primarily by retired persons, who bring a lifetime of experience and organization to their work (and who are forgiving of occasional lapses of memory and slow-moving colleagues). Is it any wonder that the most successful street ministries are staffed by people who were once on the street themselves?

During college I participated in an urban ministries program that included as one of its requirements spending a weekend on the streets of San Francisco with no money. I spent the Saturday night of that weekend at a rescue mission in the Tenderloin district. At 6:00 a.m. the next morning they kicked us all back out onto the streets. Wandering the cold downtown, I came across a homeless man huddled on the steps in front of a tenement building. He looked pretty bad; his face was bloodied in some places, and he had not washed for weeks. Coming toward me in the other direction was a well-dressed man in a leather coat. The homeless guy said, "Hey, buddy, can you spare a cigarette?" To my amazement, the well-off man pulled a cigarette out of a gold case, placed it in the man's mouth, and leaned down with his gold lighter to light the cigarette. Then he stood in silence while they both took a few puffs. When the homeless man thanked him, he responded, "Hey, no problem. I used to be on the streets myself. I know what it's like." You could write a whole book on missional Christianity based on this one story alone.

Sure, pastors and church leaders should exhort members to financially support a wide range of ministries. And obviously some stretching has to occur. If someone says he or she is only interested in sports or shopping or a particular rock band, it doesn't mean that that person's witness is limited to one of those three areas. But it also doesn't mean that the individual is going to do well working with migrant workers or in a homeless shelter. *The first step is for people to get directly involved with a community for a community* (which of course means that they have to *have* a community). When that occurs, passion-based ministry starts to happen.

You can see this model working successfully for many younger Christians in the environmental movement. As they begin to realize how urgent it is to address the problems of global climate change, they find it easier to engage in environmental activism with passion and concern. *It's not a ministry; it's a lifestyle*—there's missional Christianity in a nutshell. That's what I find so brilliant about Brian McLaren's newest book, *A New Kind of Christianity: Ten Questions That Are Transforming the Faith,* due out in February 2010. As in his previous book, *Everything Must Change*, Brian is trying to expand the range of interest and concern among American Christians. As the concerns expand, so too does the ability to engage with one's whole heart in new forms of living as a disciple.

19. Toward a Progressive Theology for Christian Activism

Now you know *how* to do it. What do the results look like? How do progressive theologies actually function? What are they based on, and what do they affirm? What can they accomplish? We will close with concrete examples of how a progressive theology can be grounded in Scripture and how it can speak powerfully and prophetically to today's world.

Why Is It Controversial for Christians to be Boldly Progressive?

There are two different senses of the word *progressive*. The broader sense of the term—changing, improving, making things better—should be uncontroversial. How could a theology not to be progressive in this sense? Our theological understanding is always evolving under the guidance of the Holy Spirit and in response to new events in human history. The sixteenth-century Reformers said that theology is *semper reformanda*, always reforming. No matter how "high" your doctrine of the Bible, it cannot mean that theology becomes static. Theologies express our ongoing attempt to interpret Scripture, our attempt to say what it means here and now—in *this* world, reacting to *these* new ideas, in conversation with *these* people, in dialogue with *this or that* world religion or philosophy. Theologies are never the absolute revelation of God, for they always includes a human dimension—the perspective of their authors.

But progressive theologies have a concrete side as well. In actual practice they always imply specific social, political, and even moral positions. Progressive theologies in this sense tend to emphasize social justice issues as strongly as they emphasize questions of individual responsibility and morality. The term is typically used of mainline Christians and "progressive evangelicals" rather than of conservatives. One would use it of President Obama but not of President Bush. One finds a broad range of organizations dedicated to supporting progressive Christianity, including many helpful web-based resources.[1]

Why has there been resistance to progressive theologies? Weren't Jesus' life and ministry boldly progressive, even revolutionary? Jesus spoke to centers of political power and took on the religious authorities of his day. He challenged the rich and powerful, placing himself consistently on the side of the poor and oppressed. He even associated the kingdom of God, which stood at the center of his teaching, with this transformation: "Blessed are you who are poor, for yours in the kingdom of God" (Luke 6:20).

One reason for the resistance, I assume, is that people read "progressive" as a code word for supporting homosexual marriages or ordaining gay clergy. At the Transforming Theology denominational summit, several denominational leaders expressed their fears that the term *progressive* has become divisive in a time when they need to be expansive. In 2009 heads of denominations—such as Katharine Jefferts Schori of the Episcopal Church of America, Mark Hanson of the Evangelical Lutheran Church of America, and Mary Hulse of the American Baptist Church—are working to prevent schism within their communions. If they identify themselves as progressive *in the narrow sense of the term*, that will be seen as a declaration of war on conservatives. By this black-and-white logic, the word *conservative* would be reduced to the sole meaning of *opposed to homosexuality*—a narrowing that should cause conservative Christians to feel equally uncomfortable.

This narrowing of Jesus' entire kingdom message to sexual ethics, and to one particular sexual issue, is immensely damaging to the gospel and the church. It is divisive to the church, distracts from her message, and is destructive to how the church is perceived in our broader society outside the church. Single-issue theologies will not transform society. Yet both sides in this damaging cultural debate are complicit in narrowing their theologies to (or toward) a single issue, at the expense of Jesus' broader message and mission.

Brian McLaren recently blogged about four major crises: the crisis of the planet, the crisis of poverty, the crisis of peace, and the crisis of purpose.[2] By

> *Jesus' ministry remained focused on the largest and most important issues.*

this last he meant "a dysfunctional spirituality system that fails to provide a framing story capable of healing the previous crises." Here are issues worthy of deep Christian attention and powerful action. When your personal reflections, and the discussions within your community, start to be obsessed with these four crises, then you know that you're devoting yourselves to issues as weighty as the ones that stood at the center of Jesus' ministry. If they *don't* preoccupy you, you're probably being distracted by the small stuff or by battles over single issues.

Social Transformation in Luke 4, Luke 6, and Matthew 25

As you pursue the "Conversations Worth Having" (see part 4), I hope you will engage in studies of Jesus' progressive message that include the entire Hebrew Bible and New Testament, the entire history of Christian thought, and the whole range of contemporary progressive theologies. There are three texts, however, to which Christians interested in social transformation return again and again and which ground our priorities. The first is Luke's account of the first act of Jesus' public ministry, in Nazareth:

> And the scroll of the prophet Isaiah was given to him. He unrolled the scroll and found the place where it was written:
>
> "The Spirit of the Lord is upon me,
> because he has anointed me
> to bring good news to the poor.
> He has sent me to proclaim release to the captives
> and recovery of sight to the blind,
> to let the oppressed go free,
> to proclaim the year of the Lord's favor." (Luke 4:17-19)

What startling words for the Son of Man to choose in order to begin his ministry! Clearly he was identifying with the Messiah, the Redeemer. But the recipients, the beneficiaries, were not what one (then or now) would expect: the poor, the prisoners, the blind, the oppressed.

The second text is Luke's account of the Beatitudes, the heart of Jesus' Sermon on the Mount:

> Looking at his disciples, he said:
> "Blessed are you who are poor,
>> for yours is the kingdom of God.
> Blessed are you who hunger now,
>> for you will be satisfied.
> Blessed are you who weep now,
>> for you will laugh.
> Blessed are you when men hate you,
>> when they exclude you and insult you
>> and reject your name as evil, because of the Son of Man.
> "Rejoice in that day and leap for joy, because great is your reward in heaven.
> For that is how their fathers treated the prophets.
> "But woe to you who are rich,
>> for you have already received your comfort.
> Woe to you who are well fed now,
>> for you will go hungry.
> Woe to you who laugh now,
>> for you will mourn and weep.
> Woe to you when all men speak well of you,
>> for that is how their fathers treated the false prophets." (Luke 6:20-26 NIV)

Again we have a key moment in Jesus' ministry. Here, more clearly than at Nazareth, Jesus preached an upside-down gospel, a gospel of reversal. The kingdom of God he came to proclaim is a kingdom of complete social transformation. The rich and well-fed have nothing in this kingdom. Its blessings come to the poor and hungry, those who weep and are despised (as the Son of Man will eventually be also).

The third text, the most staggering of all, is Jesus' last parable in Matthew. Jim Wallis calls it his "conversion text," and he is not alone:[3]

> When the Son of Man comes in his glory, and all the angels with him, he will sit on his throne in heavenly glory. All the nations will be gathered before him, and he will separate the people one from another as a shepherd separates the sheep from the goats. He will put the sheep on his right and the goats on his left.
> Then the King will say to those on his right, "Come, you who are blessed by my Father; take your inheritance, the kingdom prepared for

you since the creation of the world. For I was hungry and you gave me something to eat, I was thirsty and you gave me something to drink, I was a stranger and you invited me in, I needed clothes and you clothed me, I was sick and you looked after me, I was in prison and you came to visit me.

Then the righteous will answer him, "Lord, when did we see you hungry and feed you, or thirsty and give you something to drink? When did we see you a stranger and invite you in, or needing clothes and clothe you? When did we see you sick or in prison and go to visit you?"

The King will reply, "I tell you the truth, whatever you did for one of the least of these brothers of mine, you did for me."

Then he will say to those on his left, "Depart from me, you who are cursed, into the eternal fire prepared for the devil and his angels. For I was hungry and you gave me nothing to eat, I was thirsty and you gave me nothing to drink, I was a stranger and you did not invite me in, I needed clothes and you did not clothe me, I was sick and in prison and you did not look after me."

They also will answer, "Lord, when did we see you hungry or thirsty or a stranger or needing clothes or sick or in prison, and did not help you?"

He will reply, "I tell you the truth, whatever you did not do for one of the least of these, you did not do for me."

Then they will go away to eternal punishment, but the righteous to eternal life." (Matt. 25:31-46 NIV)

We do not have to fight over the more general issues: When does Jesus "come in glory"? Is hell literal or figurative? This parable, coming at the end of Jesus' teaching ministry and couched in terms of ultimate judgment, could not be more emphatic. The one who "sits on his throne in heavenly glory" does not just identify with, relate to, or love the needy. He claims to *be* the needy: "*I* was hungry . . . *I* was thirsty . . . *I* was a stranger . . . *I* was sick . . . *I* was in prison." Equating himself with the lowest of the low, Jesus offered his most-radical-ever statement about what the kingdom of God is and requires. The only moment in the New Testament that's more radical is the crucifixion—the steps toward which begin, according to Matthew, immediately after Jesus told this parable.

This central New Testament text begs to be thought through theologically. Its essential structure is echoed in the earliest Christian hymn, the narrative of Christ's self-emptying (Philippians 2) that we examined earlier.

In both texts the One who is exalted as the highest *actually becomes* the lowest. What is the Christ? He is the one who, humbling himself, identifies with those who have the least. He lives and acts *for them*—indeed, so radically that he becomes indistinguishable from them. "Whatever you did for one of the least of these brothers of mine, you did for me." I challenge you to begin to think through the implications of this act of complete identification for *each* of the Seven Core Christian Questions: not only for the doctrines of God, Christ, and Spirit, but also for your understanding of humanity, salvation, the church, and the nature of the Christian hope for the future. What you'll find, I suggest, is the basis for a powerful, biblically based, world-transforming, progressive theology.

 ## Working with God for the Salvation of the World

Many of us grew up in a world where you talked about *either* salvation *or* social justice. The problem is "sin, not skin"—or so I was taught at a mostly black, conservative church I attended during college. Well, here's what the new progressives are saying: *you no longer have to choose*. The problem is both sin *and* skin (racism). And the full Christian answer involves both salvation *and* social justice. (Brian McLaren and Chuck Gutenson work out this both/and beautifully in a rich online discussion of the gospel and social justice.[4]) Why did we ever think that we faced a forced choice between them?

Here's a case in point: the heading for this section comes from one of the leading progressive theologians in the country, John Cobb, addressing one of the most liberal denominations, the United Church of Christ (UCC). This talk, given only a few weeks ago (and now available online[5]), powerfully conveys progressive theology without liberal*ism*. There is no more fitting capstone for this book. With John's permission, I have generalized his references to the UCC to the church as a whole. This prophetic call opens with the words:

> My challenge can be put very simply. I am proposing that the church take as its mission working with God for the salvation of the world. The proposal makes many assumptions. First, it assumes that the world needs saving. . . . A second assumption is that God cares about the salvation of the world. This is an assumption that is made implicitly by all who pray the Lord's prayer. We ask that God's will be done on earth.

> Having learned to pray this way from Jesus, it is hardly possible to think
> that God's will for the world is immense destruction and suffering. . . .
> A third assumption is that God is already working in and through crea-
> tures, and especially human beings, toward the salvation of the world.

It's not that "salvation" means *less* than it once did; we now realize that it
means more. Sin continually separates us from God; we fall short of God's
call to us; without God's grace in Christ, the church affirms, we are unable
to heed the call to love. But the human destruction of the natural world now
means that we must work (with God) to save nature as well—just as we
must work to right the injustices that have been built into our social structures, the injustices that directly produce unspeakable suffering for other
human beings.

Cobb affirms that God is already working in and through creatures. But
he does not affirm "supernatural interpretations of historical events, or . . .
that any part of the biblical record is necessarily inerrant, or . . . that there
are no other sources of wisdom."[6] He strives for a theology that is consistent
with science and not dismissive of other religions and philosophies. Yet the
resulting theology is robust enough to speak unapologetically of working
for the salvation of the world. It's also ready to affirm the unique value of
Christianity:

> Of the world's religions, Christianity has the tradition that points most
> strongly to efforts to save the world. . . . Christians and post-Christian
> secularists have been the most important actors on the world scene in
> recent centuries, and just for this reason we Christians have special
> responsibility for dealing positively with the world's problems. Also, his-
> torical consciousness is crucial for wise direction of efforts today, and
> this has been honed most among us.[7]

In recent years Christian churches have been losing the battle of signifi-
cance. For many people, it seems less and less important to meet together
with other Christians. Pastors have built mega-churches by offering people
what they already want: the promise of financial success, of friends and community, of feeling good. But mainline churches are not convincing society,
or even their own members, that when Jesus' followers are involved with
others in missional living, they're dealing with the most significant thing in
their entire life.

The more progressive denominations on the whole have been losing members and resources. There are many reasons. But I think the deepest one may be that what we do and say does not seem to be terribly important. This is true with regard to our children whom we bring up in the church. They may have a positive attitude toward it, but they may not see any reason to give much, if any, of their time and energy to its support.[8]

Imagine what would happen if people became convinced that the biggest, most important vision for the future of humanity and the planet was the one that they found in progressive groups and churches, and that nothing else in their lives was as important. Imagine what would happen if they felt that the values that exceeded all others in importance were taught and lived paradigmatically in these Christian communities. Imagine that governments, universities, and social organizations paled in comparison. Would we not see a flow of committed people, bringing their best energy and effort to learning, preparing, and acting on behalf of this vision?

> What is needed is an inclusive vision of what the world must be in order that there be a healthy survival. We need a careful appraisal of the many threats we face in relation to that goal as well as of the existing efforts to deal with these threats. We need to be guided into seeing what changes and what new ventures would be most promising for redirecting the whole into more sustainable and regenerative channels.[9]

But this *is* the Christian vision. It's a vision of people finding reconciliation with God and with each other; people not afraid to bring this vision into dialogue with the best of the world's science, philosophy, and religion; people whose calling it is to work (with God) for the salvation of this planet and all its inhabitants. It's Jesus' vision of the kingdom of God.

> Let us suppose that the church became visible in our society as the place where the broadest vision of what needs to happen could be found. Let us suppose that people had some confidence that this vision was being constantly honed and its implications for action reformulated as the global situation changed.[10]

A moment's reflection, and a touch of humility, reminds us of how deeply we are the products of our background and culture. My vision for a both/and form of Christian theology and proclamation would not have seen the light of day without years of immersion in evangelical schools, followed by years of work among progressive Christians.

But all of us are children of our age as well. This book was born during the last months of Barack Obama's historic campaign for president. Some of the most heartfelt passages were written through a blur of tears as I watched this inspiring leader first accepting the election results and then being inaugurated as our nation's first black president. My call to a critical, reflective faith echoes Obama's moving call at the 2004 Democratic Convention in Boston, as he proclaimed that "religious commitment did not require me to suspend critical thinking, disengage from the battle for economic and social justice, or otherwise retreat from the world that I knew and loved."[11] Obama's progressive vision rocked the nation in 2008, exactly forty years after an equally gifted black leader, Martin Luther King Jr., presented a prophetic Christian vision for change that transformed American society forever.

Yet these pages are finally being published not in the months of great vision and hope—yes we can, yes we can—but in a season of rapidly hardening realism, if not outright cynicism. If there's one place on earth that eats up idealism and spits out cynicism, it's Washington D.C. One by one, the president's agendas for change, which expressed the dreams of millions of Americans, are being ground to dust. Compromise after compromise follows, leading gradually to death by a thousand qualifications. Obama's conservative opponents openly and proudly admit that their primary goal is to destroy him. With Langston Hughes we ask, "What happens to a dream deferred? Does it dry up like a raisin in the sun?"[12]

In this season of disappointment, readers may ask, "Is it also so with the dreams for the church? Will our vision of 'rekindling theological imagination' die as quickly as the dream of a Washington in which the spirit of collaboration and change triumph over 'business as usual'?" The question is fair. Clearly, as much is at stake for the mainline church today as is at stake for America under this administration. We hover on the edge of a great "tipping point," after which the sustaining institutions of mainline Christianity will begin to close and massive numbers of congregations will be no more. Is it our fate, too, to dry up like a raisin in the sun?

But the situation is *not* the same. An administration lasts for four short years. It can be brought to a standstill by voter apathy and selfishness, by the media's spin, and by an opposing party bent only on destruction. But God is from everlasting to everlasting. The great vision we have been exploring—the vision for the salvation of the world—will not go away in four years. As long as there are human beings, there will be some who refuse to be ruled by self-ishness and short-sightedness, some who put the kingdom of God ahead of all other goals. Cynicism may arise like a virus among the middle aged, but there will always be some who are ready to give their lives for Jesus' Great Reversal: "Your sons and your daughters shall prophesy, your old men shall dream dreams, and your young men shall see visions" (Joel 2:28).

For many of us, this is a time of great optimism. Complacency is the church's greatest enemy, and few people who have their eyes open today are complacent. At no time since Augustine and the Fall of Rome in the fifth century has the church stood before such revolutionary change. Many well-worn practices will be abandoned, and many beloved congregations will close. But the Spirit of God will continue to move upon the face of the waters.

So I call the courageous and faithful back to theology—to give an account of their deepest Christian commitments and their relevance for our day. No narrow theologizing will do. It's not enough just to justify existing practices, to make one's own in-group comfortable at the expense of all the rest. This new theology, genuinely transformative theology, calls for deep personal involvement, openness to criticism and new information, engage-ment with the world as it really is and with other persons as they really are. It calls for the courage to be unsure, to question, to know when to say, "I don't know." Above all, it calls for the most comprehensive and transform-ing vision that your mind can contain and your heart can dream—the vision of the coming kingdom of God. Would anything less be worthy of the One who calls us, the One who emptied himself, even Jesus of Nazareth?

Part Four

Conversations Worth Having

Transforming Christian Theology does not seek to have the last word. It's meant to function as the invitation to a passionate dialogue about theology and the way it shapes our life together as individuals and the church. Just because we do not offer a theology for you to sign on to does not mean we don't have beliefs. Sure, we have our own convictions, but more than that we believe in God's transformative presence and power in open, honest, and passionate conversations about God, Christ, and the World. We do believe that you do not have to be conservative to have Christian convictions, talk about them, and live out of them. We do believe that being followers of Jesus can create a tent big enough to embrace and partner with each other through theological difference. We do believe that a church that engages its head in theology will have a more vibrant heart, compassionate hands, and holistic life.

We believe these things, while understanding faith as being much more than the truths to which one assents. For too long we have fought over how small or large the theological requirements for essential Christianity should be. All the while, fewer and fewer committed churchgoing Christians were involved in the conversation. Sure, we did a good job teaching people how to dismiss those on the other side of the theological spectrum without much effort, but we rarely opened the theological discourse to all who would gather. Today there is a growing indifference to theological reflection in many congregations; more and more of our stances within the church and toward society are determined through other means. How do we make theology more than the gateway into the church and allow it to be a catalytic conversation among the church? How do we shift the focus of theology from particular answers for every question to particular questions for every Christian?

Conversation. It is our desire that theology—real, robust theology—be the work of the people. To do this, the church has to get over its outsourcing problem. The church can no longer let academia do its theology, the progress of culture its ethics, and a political party its activism. Theology needs to be back into the hands of the people where the consensus of convictions can transform individuals and communities to transform the church and society.

We have concluded this book with some questions and guidelines for discussion that we call "Conversations Worth Having." Hopefully these discussion starters can serve to foster transformative dialogue within your own faith community. There is much in the book that is not covered here, but these three conversations hopefully will begin a conversation that will continue to transform the life of the church and its living in and for the world. Do visit our webpage, www.transformingtheology.org, to share your feedback and find more resources from Transforming Theology, including more "Conversations Worth Having" questions, background resources, and free conversation-starting videos from more than thirty different theologians.

Conversation 1. Choice, Convictions, and Connections

I n his upcoming book, *American Grace: How Religion is Reshaping Our Civic and Political Lives*, Robert Putnam demonstrates how, from the 1990s to today, the polarization and politicizing of religion has led an increasing number of young people to reject religion and its institutions, generally taking the attitude, "If this is religion, I'm not interested."[1] The result of these overly politicized forms of faith is two generations of adults in which 30 to 35 percent are religiously unaffiliated, and a batch of kids growing up in homes with a stronger commitment to religious cynicism than life-shaping convictions offered by religiosity. Our contemporary context presses us to ask questions about the impact of religious choice, the nature of religious convictions, and how we facilitate connections in religious communities.

 ## Choice

Contemporary religious diversity is not bound to one expression of religion, even if you expand the options to include all the Abrahamic monotheisms, or even theism in general. The world's faith traditions are no longer just present in apologetic handbooks, but also in our neighborhoods and on our computer screens. The sheer plurality of religion has moved from a topic in religious studies classes to an actual characteristic of culture. We live and breathe religious pluralism. The result is a Baskin-Robbins-like selection of living religious and spiritual options.

- How have you handled religious diversity in your life? What questions has it pressed upon you?

- What impact has religious diversity made on your Christian convictions and how you hold them?
- How is this situation affecting faith in the home? What is faithful parenting in a pluralistic world, in an interfaith home?
- In what ways is the diversity of spiritual expressions an asset to faith development? When can it be a hindrance?

Convictions

Putnam calls the religiously unaffiliated, "nones." Interestingly, this group of people is not anti-religious or anti-spiritual, but simply apathetic when it comes to the dominant forms of organized religion. What they refuse to be affiliated with are the polarizing and politicizing of religious convictions at the expense of people. If religious organizations have come to represent those who use God to support their own ideology and divide people based on their own assessment of righteousness, then it makes sense that the institutions, which were once spiritual homes for many in past generations, are failing to connect in such a powerful way today.

- How can we have convictions without demonizing those who are different or becoming indifferent to convictions themselves?
- Against whom does your community define itself? What convictions are communicated in the average worship service?
- How would you state your faith in the positive and on its own terms?
- What truth has transformed your life in such a way that you see it as a gift to share with your family?

Connections

For a growing number of Americans, the church and its steeples no longer represent a harbor of safety and encouragement to the community. More importantly, the church is failing to be a place that actually contributes to people's spiritual journeys. If people neither see nor experience real redeeming connections and relationships in the religious community, if they fail to find support to self, home, and society there, then one can hardly expect them to come. Since these connections and relationships between God, each other, and the world have been the foundation of the church and our own experience within it, we need to explore how to create a space hospitable to new people finding the same life-giving connections.

- Where in your own life are you free to be open, honest, and even vulnerable?
- What has nurtured the most authentic relationships in your life?
- Where do you partner with others to make an impact in your community and in the world?
- How can your faith community support and join networks of spiritual friendship and community transformation?

Framing the Challenge Theologically

At the heart of the present discussion are our shared convictions—those beliefs that we hold so dear that they shape our dreaming, living, and dying. Our convictions shape how we interpret and engage the pluralism of our world. Likewise, it's our convictions that create communities where personal and social transformation will or will not occur. It is therefore essential to wrestle with our convictions in order to own them and to live with integrity within them as we engage our world today. To avoid the hard work of thinking through our own convictions will continue to lead the church toward irrelevancy.

- Who is God and where is God in a community that contains all the world's religious traditions?
- What would it mean to be distinctively Christian without being exclusive? To be spiritually open without being relativistic?
- What hurdles does your community face in articulating a vibrant and plausible faith?
- How can we as Christians learn from other faiths in friendships, homes, and churches?

Conversation 2. Barriers to Belonging

D enominational Christianity in America no longer functions as the thoroughfare of Christianity, or even spirituality, in the ways that it once did. Like the great American car industry in Detroit, the denominations have found themselves no longer to be the only game in town. In fact, many other forms of faith community have gradually been gaining a bigger share of the spiritual marketplace. The diversification of the market isn't necessarily a bad thing; it is simply the context.

Since the government will not be passing any denominational bailouts to keep the steeples and stained glass around, it's all the more urgent that denominations and their congregations actively engage the challenges before them. As the church is transitioning, we need to examine the cultural barriers between our congregations and the communities in which they live.

- What creates unnecessary dissonance between our congregations and their surrounding communities?
- What in our structures and programs adds distance between the church and those it seeks to invite into its community or to join in its ministry and service?
- What are the barriers that others find to belonging?

Let's think through the barriers.

 ## The Church Is Socially De-centered

Socially, we no longer expect to be asked the question, "What church do you go to?" These days we are more likely to hear, "So are you religious or spiritual or something?" The church has moved from being one of the centerpieces of society to one among many spiritual communities and personal affiliations. In the past the church was part of the cultural bedrock and served as an essential part of one's social network, performing many civic and economic functions beyond the religious. But today it is no longer necessary. Since the church is no longer at the center of the town square, we must expect that "business as usual" will continue to isolate and disconnect us from the town that has moved on without us. For many, the church has become a museum of belief, merely preserving the artifacts that were central to its previous role. For example, we continue performing rites such as baptisms, weddings, and funerals along with celebrating certain dates that remain important culturally, but we do so without nesting these rites and times in the shared convictions of the surrounding community. There once was a time when these functions were integral to society, but that is no longer the case.

A socially de-centered church is only a problem if we continue to operate as if we are still in the center of society. The church, however, has not been replaced by some other institutional center. Instead of individuals joining communities as they once did to find a network of friends, partners, and support, individuals themselves are networking through a variety of means to create their own network. Through interest groups, work, online social networking, local advocacy, school, or neutral locations such as a coffee shop or bar, people are creating personal networks that gradually become the centering community of their lives. As this becomes increasingly common, the church will have to figure out how to participate redemptively in the creation and encouragement of these networks rather than being the sole provider of them.

- When and how does your religious and spiritual life come up in conversation? What does this reveal about how your culture locates the church?
- Think of people you know who were married in a church while lacking any significant attachment to a congregation. Why did they want a church wedding? How does the meaning they give the ceremony differ from the meaning that the church gives it?
- List five friends who know what you are passionate about and who encourage your pursuits. How do you know them and where do you share with each other? Do you find similar support within the church? Why or why not?
- To what different networks of people are you connected? How does your participation in the church connect to these other

networks, and what could the church do to engage redemptively a greater number of the networks in which its members live?

The Church Is a Spiritually Ambiguous Community

One thing that is not waning today is spirituality. In fact, there are many indicators that people are becoming more open and investing more time in connecting to something Ultimate. Yet one of the last places people think of turning to for these needs is the church. Those of us who are committed to the life of the church could be tempted to respond cynically and label the variety of spiritual expressions and experiments mystical hedonism (which is often done). But doing so would not allow us to reflect on just what it means that there is growing interest and searching for the holy that is taking place outside the church walls. If anything, it should signal to us that the church is spiritually ambiguous. Many people no longer assume that the church can contribute something to their spiritual journey. For some, the idea of visiting a church would be a waste of time; for others, it would be a last resort. In any case, the cultural expectations of the church contributing to one's spiritual existence are not high. No congregation can be everything for everyone, but surely the Christian tradition and the members of our congregations have treasures worth sharing.

- What is being communicated when people identify themselves as "spiritual but not religious?" How does this sentiment resonate with you?
- How does your congregation currently contribute to, distract from, or ignore parts of your spirituality?
- Describe the diversity of spiritual practices and outlets that your friends practice.
- What is a way your congregation can invite people into a more vibrant spiritual existence?

The Church Has a "Leave it to Beaver" Bias

"Leave it to Beaver," the black-and-white television family sitcom from the 1950s, presented the traditional American family. The Cleavers were the perfect suburban family with two parents running a one-income home filled with all the Boy Scouts and apple pie a family could muster. The Cleaver family is no longer an American ideal and is becoming less frequent with each passing generation. Yet, there are many churches whose programs are geared toward Cleaver-like families. What has changed? More people are growing up in homes with single parents, living between two homes, with step-parents and step-siblings, or in a home with a same-sex couple. It is rare that a family can manage having only one employed parent, and the age at which people get married and then have kids continues to rise. Increasingly, people are choosing singleness or cohabitation outside of marriage, which creates new varieties of adult populations. On top of all this, our college students today are graduating with more debt than ever before and entering a workforce that will more than likely require them to move locations and change careers multiple times. What does it mean to be a church with the all the current fluctuations of the family?

- How diverse are your own family's living arrangements? What about those of others in your church?
- What does it take to be involved and a leader in your congregation? How diverse is the leadership and who are missing?
- Many children and grandchildren of church leaders are opting out of church participation because they have a different calendar (for example, they may work on Sunday mornings). What is the church's responsibility to those for whom this is true? What can be done?
- Congregations have long sought to celebrate family in special ways (for example, Mother's Day). What would the celebration of other life arrangements look like?

The Church Has a Credibility Crisis

The church is no longer seen as a virtuous and vital social institution. The personal failures and tragedies of many public faces of the church are common knowledge, and the media unfortunately tend to make devout Christians the butt of jokes and examples of ignorance. Beyond the public relations problem lies a real credibility crisis. While the Boomers perhaps receive too much flack as a generation in general, the world is well aware that they had the opportunity to create a different world—a world for "the least of these."

The results are far from compelling. Instead of identifying and addressing the crises of the world, too often the gospel and call of Christ became identified with personal prosperity, entitlement, and consumerism. This may not be the complete story, but it is the one being heard by many, so it remains a barrier present in culture.

- What do you understand the most pressing concerns of the world to be? How would your peers answer this question?
- Does your faith inspire you to engage these issues? How would you share this passion as an individual and a faith community?
- Who in your congregation is already engaged in addressing these global concerns? How can your community encourage, support, and join them in their sacred activism?
- Why should our children and grandchildren become Christians and not secular or even spiritual humanists?

The Church Has a Communication Opportunity

Many mainline Protestant churches are struggling to come to grips with the revolutions that are taking place in communication. The classic modes of communication in most churches are still based in the world of Gutenberg, the world created with the advent of the printing press. Technologically speaking, however, today we have moved into a Google-shaped world. Many worship services continue to be centered on the individual consumer of texts, be they read, spoken, or sung. For example, we spend the majority of the service listening to a choir, reading a bulletin, seeing the backs of fellow worshipers' heads, while looking at and possibly listening to the educated monologue from the pulpit. By contrast, today's communication is being shaped by new technologies that center on collaboration and participation—technologies that make use of images, narratives, and art *and* that function in a context of continuous flux and change. These changes are affecting everything, from the educational system to the news media, presidential campaigns, finding a spouse, and simply staying in touch with friends. The challenge is not just how to use the new technologies effectively (though ignoring them is costly); the challenge is creating a community that communicates to, in, and eventually from a Google-shaped world.

- How has the use of new technology changed your life? How has it changed the shape of your communication with and expectations of others?
- What are some examples of Gutenberg-shaped communication in your congregation? How can this be expanded or reshaped to communicate in a Google-shaped world?
- Describe the Christian story as expressed in your congregation. How are people invited to participate, transform, and express this story?
- If no one could receive a word of language in your worship service written, spoken, or sung, what would be communicated? How would you communicate the good news without words?

Framing the Conversation Theologically

If you take a look at these barriers, they are not related to theological content. They are primarily institutional in nature. That isn't to say there aren't hard theological questions that are more pressing today than at other points in church history or ones that must be taken up again because of our new situation; religious pluralism is such an example. Yet most progressive Christians have wrestled with many of these issues. Progressives seem to have in our DNA the tenacity to continue to transform our theology as we come to understand God and creation differently. And yet, the theological challenge beneath these methodological barriers is in fact deep:

- What is it that keeps many of those who are creative theologically from being creative with their practices and proclamation?
- In many ways the church in America is divided into two groups. There are those who are conservative and not open to the transformation of their message but who will employ all kinds of creative methods when it comes to getting their message out. Then there are the more progressive Christians who creatively transform their message but are generally less exploratory in their methods. What would it take to become a people so passionately committed to the living God that we have the courage to transform both our message and our method as we move into a new world?

Conversation 3. Toward a Progressive Missiology

What's our mission as the church? Theologian John Cobb believes it to be, "working with God for the salvation of the world."[2] That is one serious task. But to really understand our mission we need to move past a couple possible misunderstandings. Some could hear "salvation of the world" within a colonial framework and think we should take the truth that we possess and give it to others in order to make them "saved," just like us. This is not the case. Instead of possessing the truth, we are to be shaped by it and called to live redemptively within it. Others could assume a very narrow definition of salvation, thinking that the only problem the world has is its own individual separation from God. While the brokenness of individuals is clearly something God intends to heal, more than that is needed as we look at nations suffering from war, a planet suffering from our exploitation, and more than a billion hungry people suffering under the tyranny of a system that has forgotten them. In this world of broken persons, peoples, and planet, our God is living, present, and active on a mission for the salvation of the world. We are called join in.

Expanding the Horizon of God's Mission

The church in America has long been divided about the nature of God's mission in the world. Just think about the debates over the kingdom of God. It can be interpreted as a possibility for the present or the future of our world, it can be a message for individuals or nations, or it can be about redemption or a call to justice. There are so many ways by means of which to reduce the mission of God to something manageable, saying it is either solely about this or that. But in doing so we actually move against the trajectory of Jesus' own mission. He expanded the mission so that it included those with physical and spiritual burdens. His mission put him in conflict with the religious, social, and political authorities. Jesus and his movement called people to personal and social transformation. His movement did not monopolize God's mission but directed people towards it, and at the end of his ministry he sent his disciples out into the world to make more disciples of this way and this movement.

- What fears or concerns come to mind when you hear the word *mission*?
- Do you ever use the word *mission*? How would you define it for yourself and your faith community?
- In part 3 there is a discussion of Jesus' own description of his mission based on Luke 4, 6, and Matthew 25. Look through these passages and craft a mission statement for disciples in the way of Jesus.
- With Jesus' mission statement in mind, assess your own life mission and the mission of your church. Where do they cohere? In what ways could you expand the mission of your church? What would it look like in your situation?

A Mission of Impartial Love

An essential part of a progressive missiology is the ability and willingness to internalize the impartiality of God's love. Impartial love does not mean a blind affirmation of all actions, systems, and structures that might be considered Christian; nor does it mean a harsh application of general principles to judge others. It is, however, a departure from the "Us versus Them" mentality that has plagued the church through its history. As David Ray Griffin puts it:

> What this doctrine of God's impartial love implies is that God's unhappiness with some people's lives does not involve hate. It implies that we cannot translate our hatred into divine hatred and thereby justify and reinforce it. It implies that, when we find ourselves fighting against other people, we are fighting against people whom God loves as much as us. It implies that we cannot justify and reinforce our own indifference

to some people's welfare by assuming divine indifference. In brief, it implies that there can be no divine sanction for the typical bipolar, imperialistic viewpoint, which divides the world into the favored saints and the hated enemy, with the rest of the world being a matter of indifference except insofar as it figures into the bipolar battle.[3]

- Have you experienced the bad side from someone's partial love? Have you hurt people because of your own partiality? What is communicated in these experiences?
- When have you encountered an "Us versus Them" notion of Christian love? What justified it? How would practicing impartial love transform the situation?
- Are there ideas, people, or movements that make you question the impartiality of God's love? Where do these feelings come from?
- Griffin notes that impartial love cannot justify and reinforce our own indifference to other people's welfare. Where do you as an individual and church struggle to practice this unbounded love? What can you do to change this?

A Mission of Inverted Power

Power takes many forms and many shapes for a variety of purposes. There is military power, political power, rhetorical power, financial power, people power, and informational power. These forms of power take a variety of shapes, shapes as different as those who build crosses and those who bear them. Joining God's mission should dramatically change our relationship with power when compared with the prevailing vision of power. As Jesus told his disciples, "You know that among the Gentiles those whom they recognize as their rulers lord it over them, and their great ones are tyrants over them. But it is not so among you; but whoever wishes to become great among you must be your servant, and whoever wishes to be first among you must be slave of all" (Mark 10:42-44). Jesus not only taught an alternative vision of power, but he embodied it throughout his life and death and called his disciples to follow by taking up their own crosses.

- What forms of power do you have? What shape do they take in your life? How is power at play in your family, work, church, and nation?

- Contrast the dominant shape of power today with that to which Jesus calls his disciples. What is most striking and most challenging for you?

- The Apostle Paul described the self-emptying love of God revealed in Christ in the Philippians 2 hymn, which Philip discussed at length in chapter 13 of this book. Paul prefaced the hymn by saying, "Let the same mind be in you that was in Christ Jesus . . . ." Philip gives examples of his own struggle to live out of this mind. Describe your own understanding of this consciousness and the challenges you face in embodying it.

- How can your faith community present Jesus' inverted shape of power? What are some ways your congregation can join God's self-giving mission?

 ## Grounding our Mission Theologically

Before John Cobb gave his challenge for the church to join God in working to save the world, he stated his theological assumptions up front: the world needs saving, God cares about the salvation of the world, God is already working in and through creatures toward the salvation of the world, and there is some very important work to be done that is not now being done.[4] Relational theologians believe that these assumptions are important to a vibrant progressive understanding of mission. But more than that, they are foundational to the movement of God, still present today, proclaimed in Scripture. By looking at the major motifs of transformation in Scripture, individuals and congregations can begin to see the connections between God's collaborative works of salvation then and now. Our tradition proclaims the stories of God liberating people from bondage, bringing people home from exile, forsaking all that is God's alone and becoming vulnerable for love's sake, and making new creation a possibility in the face of sin and death. These stories run throughout Scripture in the history of Israel, the life and ministry of Jesus, and the gospel proclamation of the early church. Our challenge is not simply to proclaim these stories but to join the God who continues to seek these pathways of transformation.

- Describe the relationship between God and the world implied by Cobb's assumptions. How familiar is this relational vision? In what ways could you become more aware of God's presence and call in your daily life?

- The four transformative motifs mentioned above can be applied to individuals and groups. For example, an individual could be in bondage to a drug addiction and need liberation, as well as those trapped in the underground sex-trade in our communities. Think of real life examples of these motifs and reflect on how you could participate with God in transforming them? What practical ways can these stories be proclaimed in your congregation so they are heard as invitations to join God in God's mission? Does this more robust understanding of God's mission change the role, audience, and goal of an invitation?

Notes

Introduction

1. Marjorie Hewitt Suchocki, *God, Christ, Church: A Practical Guide to Process Theology* (New York: Crossroad, 1989), 33.

2. Brian McLaren, *Church on the Other Side* (Grand Rapids, Mich.: Zondervan, 2000), 71. Brian writes of this radical change: "It will require that Christian theologians become more like the best artists and scientists—passionately devoted to truth, and less like politicians—concerned about institutions and alliances and re-election (tenure) and book sales. I am an amateur pastor and a hack theologian, but I care about truth, and I try to think from time to time. If these lines of thought seem important to me, how much more should they inspire those with the primary calling to theology? May God give them the courage to step out of the boat and walk on water. To lead the way in our journey to the other side" (71).

3. John B. Cobb Jr., *Reclaiming the Church: Where the Mainline Church Went Wrong and What to Do about It* (Louisville: Westminster/John Knox, 1997), 5. Subsequent page numbers are included in the text.

4. The full text of this blog appears at <http://clayton.ctr4process.org/2008/09/>.

Chapter 1: Things Have Changed, or "Toto, We're Not in Kansas Any More"

1. Will Herberg, *Protestant, Catholic, Jew: An Essay in American Religious Sociology* (Garden City, N.Y.: Doubleday, 1955), 59.

2. Ibid, 59-60.

3. "U.S. Religious Landscape Survey," Pew Forum on Religion and Public Life (Washington D.C: Pew Research Center, 2008), 5. Page numbers for subsequent statistics from this study are noted within the text.

4. Associated Press, "Southern Baptist Membership, Baptisms Decline" (April 24, 2008), http://www.ajc.com/news/content/news/stories/2008/04/24/southernbaptists_0424 .html (accessed July 1, 2009).

5. See http://www.beliefnet.com/Entertainment/Quizzes/BeliefOMatic.aspx (accessed July 19, 2009).

Chapter 2: Do Christians Have to Hate Change?

1. See the beautiful chapter, "The church in, with, against, and for the world," in Doug Ottati, *Reforming Protestantism: Christian Commitment in Today's World* (Louisville: Westminster/John Knox, 1995).

2. Don Schlitz, "The Gambler," 1978.

Chapter 4. Postmodernity Makes Theologians of Us All

1. Louis Dupré, *Passage to Modernity: An Essay in the Hermeneutics of Nature and Culture* (New Haven: Yale University Press, 1993).

2. In books like *Erring: A Postmodern A/theology* (Chicago: University of Chicago Press, 1987), Mark L. Taylor defines Derrida's post-structuralism in terms of a four-fold death: the death of God, the death of the subject, the death of the author (and hence the book), and the death of history. In chapter 16 of *Adventures in the Spirit* (Minneapolis: Fortress Press, 2008) I've argued that Derrida's position on God, especially toward the end of his life, is rather more subtle.

3. I'm now working on a book on this topic, tentatively entitled *This Sacred Earth: Why Religious Partnerships are Indispensable to Economic, Ecological, and Social Sustainability.*

4. Roger Haight, *The Future of Christology* (New York: Continuum, 2005), 128-129.

Chapter 5: Postmodern Believing

1. Carl F. H. Henry (1913–2003), the first dean of Fuller Theological Seminary and the founder of *Christianity Today*, is considered by many to be the father of neo-evangelicalism.

2. Gary Gutting, *Religious Belief and Religious Scepticism* (Notre Dame, Ind.: Notre Dame University Press, 1982), 107.

3. Ibid, 108.

4. Jane Chamberlain and Jonathan Rée, eds., *The Kierkegaard Reader* (Oxford: Black-well, 2001), 248.

5. John Rae, *Martin Luther: Student, Monk, Reformer* (London: Hodder and Stoughton, 1896), 276.

Chapter 6: "Everything Must Change"

1. Brian D. McLaren, *Everything Must Change* (Nashville: Thomas Nelson, 2007), 2-3.

2. Ibid, 3.

3. http://news.cnet.com/8301-1035_3-10048257-94.html (accessed July 20, 2009).

4. http://www.apostleschurch.org/home.php (accessed July 20, 2009).

5. http://www.freshexpressions.org.uk/index.asp?id=1 (accessed July 20, 2009).

6. http://www.youtube.com/watch?v=a3Vy2V0QwuA (accessed July 20, 2009).

Chapter 9. Transformative Theologies

1. Peter Berger has beautifully (and prophetically) described this dilemma between the two sides in his book, *A Far Glory* (New York: Anchor Books, 1993).

Chapter 10. Learning to Find Your Theological Voice

1. http://www.saddleback.com/aboutsaddleback/whatwebelieve/index.html (accessed July 24, 2009).

2. Bruce Sanguin's interview is at http://homebrewedchristianity.com/2008/10/02/the-emerging-church-with-bruce-sanguin-homebrewed-christianity-ep26/ (accessed July 24, 2009).

3. Martin Luther, The Ninety-Five Theses. These quotations are from the Wittenberg website, Luther.de, and can be found at http://www.luther.de/en/95thesen.html (accessed July 24, 2009).

Chapter 11: Theology as Telling the Story

1. Brian McLaren, *A Generous Orthodoxy* (Grand Rapids, Mich.: Zondervan, 2004), 289.

2. I quote from the blog pre-version of Delwin Brown's new book, http://progressive theology.wordpress.com/1-rediscovering-our-progressive-christian-heritage/ (accessed June 15, 2009).

3. See my books *Mind and Emergence: From Quantum to Consciousness* (Oxford University Press, 2004); *The Re-emergence of Emergence (*co-edited with Paul Davies) (Oxford University Press, 2006); and *In Quest of Freedom: The Emergence of Spirit in the Natural World* (Göttingen: Vandenhoeck and Ruprecht, 2008).

4. See the beautiful statement of the Cedar Ridge church at http://www.crcc.org/pdfdocs/vision.pdf (accessed July 26, 2009).

Chapter 12: Theologies in Action

1. Richard Carlson, *Don't Sweat the Small Stuff. . . and it's all small stuff* (New York: Hyperion, 1997), 7.

Chapter 13: A Theology of Self-Emptying for the Church

1. Doug Pagitt, *The Emerging Church and Embodied Theology* (Grand Rapids, Mich.: Zondervan, 2007). See pp. 121-133, "Listening to the Beliefs of Emerging Churches."

2. Academic theology may require such things, but we've already seen that what academic theology requires is not always good for giving voices back to Christians at large. Also, some will say that church polity requires exact specifications of this doctrine. In this book I am suggesting that, though that has been true, it need not and should not be the starting point for talking about church today.

3. C.S. Lewis, *The Chronicles of Narnia* (New York: HarperCollins, 1954; 1982), 216.

4. It's a bit like finding the right balance between faith and works. Some congregations need to hear, "For by grace you have been saved through faith, and this not your own doing; it is the gift of God—not the result of works, so that no one may boast" (Eph. 2:8-9). Others more need to hear, "faith by itself, if it has no works, is dead" (James 2:17).

Chapter 14. New Partnerships in Christian Activism

1. The article on pragmatic idealism by Jonathan Pontell appeared in the Opinion section of *USA Today* on January 27, 2009. See http://blogs.usatoday.com/oped/2009/01/stuck-in-the-mi.html#more (accessed July 31, 2009).

2. Stephen Mansfield, "Obama's Faith Fits our Times," online at http://blogs.usatoday.com/oped/2009/06/obamas-faith-fits-our-times.html (accessed June 30, 2009).

Chapter 15. Time to Leave behind Old Liberal/Evangelical Battles

1. As Mark S. Gietzen, chairman of the Kansas Coalition for Life, put it, "The credit is going to go to him. There are people who are agreeing with him." And after the murder, Troy Newman, president of Operation Rescue, told the press that he knew well before the murder that Scott Roeder "had argued in years past that homicide was justifiable to stop abortions." See the *New York Times* feature article from July 26, 2009, at http://www.nytimes.com/2009/07/26/us/26tiller.html?_r=1&th=&adxnnl=1&emc=th&adxnnlx=1248731548-7vhaoi0BdW1/+N7Ao5t9dQ (accessed July 27, 2009).

2. Hal Taussig's article, "Grassroots Progressive Christianity: A Quiet Revolution," has been published online (along with a helpful list of discussion questions) at http://www .sdc.unitingchurch.org.au/WestarProgressiveArticle.pdf. I have quoted the summary from http://en.wikipedia.org/wiki/Progressive_Christianity (both accessed July 28, 2009).

3. Glen H. Stassen's many works include *Just Peacemaking: Transforming Initiatives for Justice and Peace* (Louisville, Ky.: Westminster John Knox, 1992); *Just Peacemaking: The New Paradigm for the Ethics of Peace and War* (Cleveland, Oh.: Pilgrim, 1998; 2004; 2008); *Living the Sermon on the Mount: A Practical Hope for Grace and Deliverance* (San Francisco: Jossey-Bass, 2006). See also his work with David P. Gushee, *Kingdom Ethics: Following Jesus in Contemporary Context* (Downers Grove, Ill.: InterVarsity, 2003) and his new book, edited with Mark Thiessen Nation, honoring John Howard Yoder, *The War of the Lamb: The Ethics of Nonviolence and Peacemaking* (Grand Rapids, Mich.: Brazos, 2009).

Chapter 16. From Church Ministries to Missional Churches

1. Tom Sine, *The New Conspirators: Creating the Future One Mustard Seed at a Time* (Madison, Wis.: InterVarsity, 2008), 39.

2. Dan Kimball, *The Emerging Church* (Grand Rapids, Mich.: Zondervan, 2003), 73.

3. Ibid, 70.

4. Eddie Gibbs and Ryan K. Bloger, *Emerging Churches: Creating Christian Community in Postmodern Cultures* (Grand Rapids, Mich.: Baker, 2005), 235 (emphasis added).

5. Ibid, 237.

6. Ibid, 19.

7. Ibid, 48.

8. See Brian McLaren's twelfth strategy, "Enter the Postmodern World," in *The Church on the Other Side: Exploring the Radical Future of the Local Congregation* (Grand Rapids, Mich.: Zondervan, 2000), p. 9.

9. I here summarize Brian's first eight strategies, together with the descriptions that he gives for each on pp. 8-9 in *The Church on the Other Side.*

Chapter 17. Social Transformation without "Us versus Them"

1. Stanley H. Skreslet, *Picturing Christian Witness: New Testament Images of Disciples in Mission* (Grand Rapids, Mich.: Eerdmans, 2006).

Chapter 18. Constructing Theologies of the Community for the Community: The Six Steps

1. Barack Obama, *The Audacity of Hope* (New York: Crown, 2006), 207.

Chapter 19. Toward a Progressive Theology for Christian Activism

1. A great list of progressive Christian websites can be found at http://www.progressive christianwitness.org/pcw.cfm?p=7(accessed July 30, 2009). Some prefer the title "New Progressives." In the (big tent) interest of finding common ground, I will not focus here on the distinctions between the various wings of progressive Christianity.

2. Brian's blog is at http://www.brianmclaren.net/archives/blog/big-publishing-news .html (accessed July 28, 2009).

3. Jim Wallis uses these words in his *Mother Jones* interview; see http://www.mother-jones.com/politics/2005/03/gods-politics-interview-jim-wallis (accessed July 28, 2009).

4. See http://imitatiochristi.blogs.com/imitatio_christi/2005/06/a_theology_for_.html (accessed July 28, 2009).

5. Cobb's challenge is posted at http://community.ucc.org/post/Groups/The_Cobb_
Challenge/blog/john_cobbs_challenge_to_the_united_church_of_christ.html?cons_id=
&ts=1249011200&signature=ceb48712c8676dbee8516ad838a8ef44 (accessed July 30,
2009).

6. Ibid.

7. Ibid.

8. Ibid.

9. Ibid.

10. Ibid.

11. Barack Obama, *The Audacity of Hope* (New York: Crown, 2006), 208.

12. Langston Hughes' famous poem has been frequently anthologized and appears
in numerous places on the web. See http://www.americanpoems.com/poets/Langston
-Hughes/2381 (accessed August 17, 2009).

Conversations Worth Having

1. Michael Gerson, "A Faith for the Nones" in *The Washington Post* (May 9, 2009), http://
www.washingtonpost.com/wp-dyn/content/article/2009/05/07/AR2009050703056
.html (accessed June 25, 2009).

2. This quotation from John Cobb is used in chapter 19 and discussed in detail on pp.
151-153.

3. David Ray Griffin, *God & Religion in the Postmodern World* (Albany: State University of New York, 1989), 144.

4. Cobb's challenge is posted at http://community.ucc.org/post/Groups/The_Cobb_
Challenge/blog/john_cobbs_challenge_to_the_united_church_of_christ.html?cons_id=
&ts=1249011200&signature=ceb48712c8676dbee8516ad838a8ef44 (accessed July 30,
2009).

For Further Reading

Bass, Diana Butler. *Christianity for the Rest of Us: How the Neighborhood Church Is Transforming the Faith.* New York: HarperCollins, 2006.

Burke, Spencer, ed. *Out of the Ooze: Unlikely Love Letters to the Church from Beyond the Pew.* Colorado Springs: Colo.: NavPress, 2007.

Cobb, John B. Jr. *Reclaiming the Church: Where the Mainline Church Went Wrong and What to Do about It.* Louisville: Westminster/John Knox, 1997.

Cowart, Courtney. *An American Awakening.* New York: Seabury, 2008.

Elnes, Eric. *The Phoenix Affirmations: A New Vision for the Future of Christianity.* San Francisco: Jossey-Bass, 2006.

Frost, Michael and Alan Hirsch, *The Shaping of Things to Come: Innovation and Mission for the 21st-Century Church.* Peabody, Mass.: Hendrickson, 2003.

Gibbs, Eddie and Ryan K. Bloger. *Emerging Churches: Creating Christian Community in Postmodern Cultures.* Grand Rapids, Mich.: Baker, 2005.

Jones, Tony. *The New Christians: Dispatches from the Emergent Frontier.* San Francisco: Jossey-Bass, 2008.

Jones, Tony and Doug Pagitt, eds. *An Emergent Manifesto of Hope.* Grand Rapids, Mich.: Baker, 2007.

Kimball, Dan. *The Emerging Church: Vintage Christianity for New Generations.* Grand Rapids, Mich.: Zondervan, 2003.

McKnight, Scot. *A Community Called Atonement.* Nashville, Tenn.: Abingdon, 2007.

McLaren, Brian D. *Church on the Other Side.* Grand Rapids, Mich.: Zondervan, 2000.

———. *Everything Must Change : Jesus, Global Crises, and a Revolution of Hope.* Nashville, Tenn.: Thomas Nelson, 2007.

————. *A Generous Orthodoxy*. Grand Rapids, Mich.: Zondervan, 2004.

Ottati, Doug. *Reforming Protestantism: Christian Commitment in Today's World*. Louisville: Westminster/John Knox, 1995.

Pagitt, Doug. *A Christianity Worth Believing: Hope-Filled, Open-Armed, Alive-and-Well Faith for the Left Out, Left Behind, and Let Down in Us All*. San Francisco: Jossey-Bass, 2008.

————. *The Emerging Church and Embodied Theology*. Grand Rapids, Mich.: Zondervan, 2007.

Rollins, Peter. *How (Not) to Speak of God*. Brewster, Mass.: Paraclete, 2006.

Sine, Tom and Shane Claiborne. *The New Conspirators: Creating the Future One Mustard Seed at a Time*. Downers Grove, Ill.: InterVarsity, 2008.

Stassen, Glen H. *Just Peacemaking: The New Paradigm for the Ethics of Peace and War*. Cleveland: Pilgrim, 1998; 2008.

————. *Living the Sermon on the Mount: A Practical Hope for Grace and Deliverance*. San Francisco: Jossey-Bass, 2006.

Tickle, Phyllis. *The Great Emergence*. Grand Rapids, Mich.: Baker, 2008.

Ward, Keith. *Re-Thinking Christianity*. Oxford, Eng.: Oneworld Publications, 2007.

Warren, Rick. *The Purpose Driven Church*. Grand Rapids, Mich.: Zondervan, 1995.

Webber, Robert, ed. *Listening to the Beliefs of Emerging Churches*. Grand Rapids, Mich.: Zondervan, 2007.